DATE DUE

← MAP OF EUROPE

Open this fold-out map to see major flight
paths, to chart your route, and to note sights
of interest that you may spot along the way.

VOLGA RIVER

Moscow

THE EAST

DNIEPER RIVER

AL EUROPE

Black Sea

THE BALKAN PENINSULA

Athens

ean Sea

WINDOW SEAT

‹ EUROPE ›

READING THE LANDSCAPE FROM THE AIR

GREGORY DICUM

CHRONICLE BOOKS
SAN FRANCISCO

Library of Congress Cataloging-in-Publication Data available.
ISBN-10: 0-8118-5151-6
ISBN-13: 978-0-8118-5151-0

Manufactured in China
Designed by Erik Olsen Graphic Design

Distributed in Canada by Raincoast Books
9050 Shaughnessy Street
Vancouver, British Columbia V6P 6E5

10 9 8 7 6 5 4 3 2 1

Chronicle Books LLC
85 Second Street
San Francisco, California 94105

www.chroniclebooks.com

ACKNOWLEDGMENTS

This flight of wonder was made all the more magnificent by the many fellow window-seaters who lent me their expertise, advice, and enthusiasm along the way.

It comes as no surprise that the people who work with satellite imagery are inveterate window gazers, and were happy to help me find the imagery in this book. I received especially indispensable help from Adam Ward at SPOT Image as well as Juliya Rubin, Stefan Patashvili, Miles Taylor, and Kirsten Kemner at GlobeXplorer.

The people at Chronicle Books have been a joy to work with once again. In particular Jodi Davis, whose commitment to window-gazing ensured that this European book followed the original title, and whose unwavering editorial eye has made this book so useful and readable. Erik Olsen's arresting design ensures you'll be proud to have the baggage inspectors flip through this book when they find it in your carry-on. Kate Prouty's light and sure touch made the complicated process move flawlessly.

The hard work of my agent, Wendy Burton Brouws, helped usher this book into the world; I am tremendously grateful for everything she does.

Nina Luttinger deserves boundless thanks. Not only did she helpfully review my work at every step of the way and energetically uncover market opportunities for the book, but she believes in it so much that she has become my coauthor on a forthcoming children's version. But even more than that, I am eternally grateful that she always lets me have the window seat.

Many thanks to Morgan Stetler, who alleviated many technical headaches along the way.

This book is better for the countless helpful comments and suggestions from readers of the first *Window Seat*. It is a pleasure to write for such sharp eyes and keen minds.

Finally, thanks to all the seatmates, cabin crews, and pilots who have answered my questions over the years, and who have helped make each and every flight an unmitigated marvel.

CONTENTS

INTRODUCTION

Taking a commercial passenger flight is one of the unheralded joys of life in the modern world. Sure, the food might be utilitarian, the seat cramped, and your neighbor annoying, but the sheer pleasure of contemplating our planet from 10 kilometers (6.5 mi., or 35,000 ft.) up in the air is worth any price. A century ago, nobody on Earth could have hoped to see this view, and yet it's yours—free—with every flight you take.

This book is not just for those of us who insist on getting the window seat every time—we who rearrange our travel schedules to guarantee daytime flights, and who look forward to an extra leg or an unplanned detour as an opportunity to examine some new territory. This book is for anyone who has glanced out the window and wondered what that strange pattern on the ground is, or why that huge building is in the middle of nowhere. This book is for the planetary explorer disguised in the ho-hum garb of the modern airline passenger.

Window Seat: Europe crams a lot of territory between its covers: Europe comprises 10.6 million square kilometers (4 million sq. mi.). Because hundreds of possible routes await you, *Window Seat: Europe* is designed to be read in many different ways. You can check the map of major routes at the front of the book to figure out what parts of the continent you will pass over on your flight, then follow along as your flight progresses. Or browse through the various sections of the book to learn more generally about what you'll be seeing along the way. Specific elements that appear frequently—in particular, human-created features like railroads and power plants—are dealt with in detail once and then cross-referenced elsewhere.

Of course, if you're already in the air, your best starting point is to skip straight to the sights you see outside your window. Come back to this introduction later, but don't waste valuable flight time here—who knows what you might be missing!

Nearly thirty thousand airline flights depart each day in Europe, making it the second-densest region of air travel on the planet. Over a billion passengers fly here each year on Europe's hundreds of high-altitude jetways. Because so many different trips are possible, this book does not focus only on specific sights. While features of note such as the Iron Curtain, Vatican City, and Loch Ness are covered, more emphasis is given to the general trends you will see on any flight through particular regions, rather than on specifics that depend on more than a little luck to spot.

You will find a variety of different resources in these pages, including maps, satellite images, and sidebars scattered throughout the book on pertinent topics from plate tectonics to smog. These will help you to chart your own path through the information here—one relevant to the specifics of your flight. Start by finding your route on the map, and figure out which parts of the continent you will be flying over. Then, look at the corresponding sections. From there, explore wherever you like.

If you are inclined to undertake more advanced window gazing, a road-map is a very handy addition to your carry-on bag. With this simple visual aid, you can keep detailed track of your route and identify specific towns and various geographical features. You can also find additional information online at www.windowseat.info.

Window Seat: Europe follows up the original *Window Seat*, which was aimed at travelers flying over North America. The success of that book uncovered a previously unappreciated subculture of hard-core window gazers— perhaps you're one of them, or soon will be. As with the first book, the goal of *Window Seat: Europe* is to help you learn to "read" the landscape that is passing below you. My hope is that for those of you who already spend your flights with your noses pressed against the window, this slim volume will further enrich the joy and wonder of gazing down from that exalted perch. For the rest of you, I hope that this book will help transform your flying hours into a sublime opportunity to understand our world as never before.

READING THE LANDSCAPE FROM THE AIR

When, as a small child, you opened a book for the first time, the writing on the pages seemed incomprehensible. But as you acquired just a little knowledge, the letters resolved themselves into words, and the words into meanings. The same goes for reading the landscape. If you know what to look for, gazing out an airplane window is like reading an ever-unfolding scroll on which is written the life-size story of the continent.

From more than 10 kilometers (35,000 ft.) in the air, the tiny details fall away. At this altitude, you can't see a particular rock or tree or street—you can see only rock and forest and roads in general. The details are fascinating in their own right, but they distract us from the larger vistas they are a part of. From outside the ordinary human scale, we can see things not normally visible to us.

This vantage point takes a little getting used to. Because people don't ordinarily view the world from this height, we need to learn a new visual vocabulary that will help us make sense of it all. Just as an individual rock, tree, or street can tell a lot about itself, including its history and the history of its place, a whole landscape of rock, forests, and roads contains volumes of information about the area and about the forces acting on it. You just have to learn the alphabet needed to read the book of the physical world spread out before you.

If you gaze out your plane window long enough, no matter what kind of landscape is below you, you'll soon spot categories of features. You'll notice mountains, rivers, forests, and towns, and you'll see that each one has distinctive characteristics. These categories of features, which geographers call layers, can be thought of as transparent maps laid down on top of one another to create the whole landscape.

The layers that are most useful in making sense of what you see out your window are, from the bottom up, rock, water, plants, and people. Each successive layer is younger and more ephemeral than the last, and dependent on the patterns of the one that precedes it for many of its features.

Imagine a mountain, tall and solid, made of pure rock. This is the first layer. Because it reaches so high, the mountain collects rainfall, and streams flow from its slopes into a lake below. This is the second layer. Because the streams and lake provide plenty of water, a forest grows. This is the third layer. Because the forest supplies wood and water is abundant, people build a town on the lake's edge. This is the fourth layer.

You can see that the characteristics of each layer inform those of subsequent layers. But there is also feedback: Streams can carve gorges into the mountainside. The growth of the forest can fill in the lake. People can clear the forest. And it goes on forever. The landscape you see from your window is a momentary snapshot of constantly changing features acting on each other. But they do so in predictable ways, and if you know a little bit about how the layers influence one another, you can read this snapshot and figure out what has been going on here over not just the past few years but also the past few thousand or even few million years.

So, first, you must be able to identify the layers. This is pretty simple; you've been doing it all your life. You can already tell mountains from forests, for example, so it's just a short leap to be able to identify these broad categories:

ROCK

Geology is rock in all its forms, which includes features like sand and mud. The underlying rock, the oldest element of a landscape, often dates back hundreds of millions of years. Though some of its elements may derive from once-living material, this rock is the result of physical and chemical processes like volcanic activity and weathering.

WATER

Water is easy to spot—it's shiny and often appears blue. When it's flowing in rivers, it forms long, often sinuous strands across a landscape. And don't forget, it can be frozen, too: Snow and ice are just water in a different form.

PLANTS

If it's green, it's probably plants. The green chlorophyll plants use to capture energy from the sun is the most readily visible evidence of life on Earth. However, not all biological elements are green, at least not all the time: Watch for earth tones like reds, yellows, and browns as well. In general, look for tufted shapes, green and tan colors, and irregular patterns that parallel geological or hydrological features.

PEOPLE

In almost every case, if you see straight lines or right angles, people are responsible for them. The same goes for perfect geometrical shapes like circles or squares. People also produce nearly all ground lights.

You'll quickly learn to tell these landscape layers apart, and you'll soon see that many elements occur in predictable combinations: Water always flows downhill, for example, and smaller rivers flow into bigger ones. You'll also notice that water attracts people—towns and all sorts of industrial facilities are usually found near a water supply.

Once you get a feel for these kinds of relationships and can make sense of what you're looking at, you'll be reading the landscape fluently. The view from the window seat will never be the same again.

The images in this book were taken by satellites orbiting many times higher than any commercial flight (so far). Though they look a little different from the views you'll see out your window, they are the best general resource for picturing our planet. The advent of satellites has changed the way we visualize the world and our place in it.

Everything you will see out your airplane window has been documented by thousands of satellite images. You can find a satellite image of nearly any place on Earth online if you know where to look. You might try starting with www.windowseat.info.

In the following pages, you'll begin to get a sense of why this imagery has had such a profound impact on our sense of place in the world. These exquisite vistas are like reports back from an exotic planet, but one that we can visit. You can take a cruise up the deep fjords of the Norwegian coast, drive around and Santiago de Compostela, trudge across the Arctic barrens, or breathe the warm, soft air of the Greek Islands.

This dynamic and relentlessly beautiful Earth is our home, and today we can appreciate it as never before: Commercial jet travel gives everyone the chance to be a planetary observer.

On a long flight you might see any of the varied faces of the European continent: the distinctive canals of Venice (above), gracefully urban density in Paris (pages 16–17), or the rugged wilderness of the Iron Gate (pages 18–19).

ATLANTIC EUROPE

THE BRITISH ISLES

FRANCE

SCOTLAND

● Edinburgh

North Sea

IRELAND

Manchester ●

Dublin ●

THE BRITISH ISLES

WALES

THAMES RIVER

ENGLAND   ● London

SEINE RIVER

Paris ●

LOIRE RIVER

Atlantic Ocean

FRANCE

ALPS

RHÔNE RIVER

PYRENEES

● Marseille

Corsic

THE BRITISH ISLES

WATCH FOR

GEOLOGICAL FEATURES

		Rugged Uplands	Gently Rolling Basins	Fjords

HYDROLOGICAL FEATURES

		Fjords	Rivers	Lakes

ECOLOGICAL FEATURES

			Heaths	Isolated Forest Patches

HUMAN FEATURES

	Fields	Sprawling Cities	Factories	Reclaimed Coastal Land

BONUS SIGHTS

Scottish Highlands, the Lake District, old factory towns, white chalk features, old airfields

The British Isles are, for many travelers to Europe, the first landfall after the long Atlantic crossing. After the empty monotony of cold blue water, the shimmering green of Ireland or Scotland is as welcome a sight as home itself.

This relatively northern part of Europe is often the first landfall precisely because of its latitude. The shortest route between any two places on the planet is known as the Great Circle route. Because it is plotted over the spherical surface of Earth, the Great Circle route can be quite different from that suggested by a flat map, particularly for places far from the equator. Accordingly, flights from North America approach the Continent from the north, rather than from the southwest as a line drawn straight eastward between nearest-seeming points on a world map would suggest.

So the first parts of Europe these travelers see are often the Caledonian Mountains of the Scottish Highlands and the Antrim Plateau in Northern Ireland. These landforms are part of an arc of old mountains that stretches from Ireland through Scotland and on into Norway, eventually reaching far

IRELAND: The rugged coast of Ireland faces the full fury of the Atlantic Ocean, but in spite of this the culture here has never been particularly seafaring. While the first humans arrived up to 7,500 years ago, during the last remnants of the Ice Age when the island was treeless arctic tundra, the land soon became thickly forested as the moist climate warmed. Later Neolithic settlers cut down the woods to create pastureland for cattle, thus establishing the windswept, green and peat-producing landscape we see today. The Irish countryside has been farmed intensively for thousands of years, yet starting with the Great (Potato) Famine in the nineteenth century, the number of people living on the land has decreased sharply. From the air, watch for abandoned farmsteads or old, disused field boundaries.

above the Arctic Circle. The rocks of this rugged belt are half a billion years old, and tectonic and glacial action has transformed them again and again—a tale told today by their rounded forms and low profiles (see Glacial Terrain, page 60, and Plate Tectonics, page 102).

The North Atlantic Drift—a "river" of warm air and ocean water that moves northeast across the Atlantic Ocean—keeps the British Isles and the rest of northwest Europe far more temperate than the high latitude would suggest: Edinburgh is farther north than Moscow, yet it rarely gets much snow. If you're flying out over the North Atlantic, take a look and see if you can spot its effects. If you look carefully, you'll notice the area between the British Isles and Iceland is largely free of the icebergs and winter ice that you'll spot farther west.

Two thousand years ago Julius Caesar wrote of Britain's "intricate and woody places," for the British Isles were once covered in heavy forest. But today much of the landscape is given over to moorlands. These open expanses of heath (low shrubs) and bog (wetlands) were created by the early inhabitants who felled the forests for fuel and building materials and then used the land to graze sheep and cattle. From above, heaths and bogs might look similarly green and featureless, but they are quite different down below: heaths often occur on rolling uplands while bogs form on bottomlands where water collects.

The forest that remains—about a tenth of the original extent—is heavily managed for timber and recreation. Indeed, there are few other places in the world where the land must meet so many competing demands. Particularly in England, every bit of space is spoken for, and any new use—such as roads and railway lines, or even changes in farming systems—must undergo a lengthy and loudly democratic process of debate.

The British love of the bucolic countryside is constantly at odds with the growth and infrastructure development inherent in a dynamic economy. The vistas of small farms and estates in the south and villages and pasture in the rockier highland areas to the north are the result of concerted efforts to preserve these landscapes. There is no longer any place in the British Isles that could properly be called wilderness. Even many national parks and other apparently "natural" areas were formed by human interaction with the land. For example,

LOCH NESS: Part of a chain of ancient mountains stretching from Ireland to Norway, the Scottish Highlands are riven with faults and carved by glaciers. Loch Ness is one such fault that has been flooded. Twenty-three miles long and a mile wide, this narrow loch (lake) fills part of the Great Glen Fault, a break between the northern and southern parts of the Scottish Highlands. This break in the rock is 400 million years old, yet is still seismically active: Small earthquakes shake the area every few decades. The present shape of this formation was carved out by a large glacier over ten thousand years ago, and other glacial landscape elements like moraines, braided streams, and eskers litter the region. Ben Nevis, the highest point in the British Isles, rises to 1,343 meters (4,406 ft.) just south of Loch Ness.

the digging of peat for fuel in the Middle Ages, followed by a subsequent rise in water table that filled the excavations, created the Norfolk Broads—the lake-dotted parkland northeast of London that is England's largest collection of wetlands.

In their settlement patterns, the British Isles are something of a microcosm of the Continent itself. They have some of the least-populated parts of Europe (Ireland), as well as some of the densest (the London Basin). Underdeveloped regions like Cornwall—the long peninsula that juts southwest toward the Atlantic—and conflict areas like Northern Ireland share the isles with metropolitan centers like the City of London.

At the southern end of the Pennine Mountains sits England's industrial heartland—the world's first industrial belt. Blessed with easily accessible surface seams of coal, this area, called the Midlands, hosted the development of large, coal-powered textile mills beginning in the eighteenth century that attracted laborers from throughout the region. In short order, industrialization depopulated the countryside and crammed workers together in the inadequate housing of company towns. The industrial effluvia of pollution and slag heaps from mining changed the pastoral landscape overnight, and an entirely new kind of human society developed.

While much industry has subsequently moved on to southern England or abroad, the story of the Industrial Revolution is written clearly on the landscape of the Midlands. Looking down from your perch high in the sky, you can detect a pattern of development that originated here nearly two centuries ago and continues to spread around the world. Watch for old factories surrounded by rows and rows of brick townhouses (though few of the original factories are in operation, and some have been revitalized as trendy postindustrial office and residential spaces).

You'll also see evidence of mining, which continues to be a core element of the British economy. The United Kingdom is visibly pockmarked with mining history. In the Midlands and in other old coal-producing areas, like Abferan in Wales, look for dark, clustered mountains of processed rock and vast pits left behind by mining (these, too, are being reclaimed, and efforts made to regreen them). Newer coal areas such as those in Yorkshire are less likely to have open pit mines, as the seams are deeper, but look for fresh mountains of tailings and, in the case of English coal mining, nearby power plants with their characteristic tall smokestacks (coal in the United Kingdom is now used mostly for the generation of electricity).

Near urban centers, watch for gravel pits, source of the raw materials for the concrete that gives cities their hard form and gray color. In Cornwall, clay mining has left behind a landscape of white hills and pools of water (known as the "Cornish Alps") around the town of St. Austell. Slate quarries, metal mines, and brickworks have all left their mark on the land over the centuries.

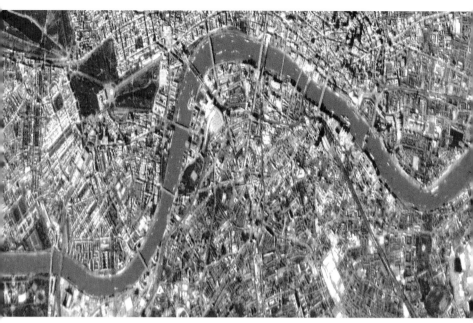

LONDON'S WEST END: For three centuries, the West End of London has been an enclave of the upper classes. As European cities industrialized and grew in the nineteenth century, coal smoke blackened the skies and ruined the health of city dwellers. Because the prevailing winds in Europe blow from the west, the western edges of cities across the continent had clearer air, and became more desirable and expensive districts. Today, even though the pollution situation is much improved, the western sides of most European cities are still more upscale, even when they have been engulfed in spreading urbanization. Here, the results are clear: compare the left of this image, with its ample parkland, large townhouses, generous greenery, and palaces (including Buckingham Palace, the official residence of the British monarch) with the dense City of London to the right, on the site of the original Roman settlement.

While some of the older industrial areas—notably Glasgow and Edinburgh in Scotland with their "Silicon Glen," a burgeoning corridor of high-tech industries—have remained important centers, others have lost out to the twentieth-century trend of economic concentration in southern England.

You'll see the results of this movement immediately when your plane arrives over the London Basin. The countryside gives way to a series of ever-larger towns that eventually merge into the London Metropolitan Area, home to 14 million people. The surrounding sprawl, arisen in spite of the best efforts of landscape conservationists and regional planners, is an example of one of the universal by-products of the advent of the automobile. The new postwar norm of private car ownership enabled commutes in all directions and permitted housing and work sites to be widely dispersed. This arc of suburban counties around the London Basin from Norfolk to Dorset is the fastest-growing part of the country.

Culturally, the London Basin dominates the United Kingdom—the "standard" English you hear on the BBC is from this region. With 90 percent of

BRACKNELL: After World War II, in an effort to reverse the long-standing trend of population concentration in sprawling London, the British Government established 28 so-called New Towns to serve as regional development centers. Few of them actually succeeded in this. Some, including many of the 14 New Towns comprising the London Ring, were subsequently overtaken by the sprawl of existing cities. Others, like Bracknell (seen here), failed to thrive and became run-down, crime-ridden dead zones (a renewed round of planning is now seeking to ameliorate these problems). From the air, typical features of New Towns include a circular shape divided into irregular neighborhoods of high rises and row houses, a car-oriented plan with lots of broad curving streets and roundabouts, leafy streets, a mall-like town center, and highway connections leading straight to London.

its population living in cities, the United Kingdom is one of the most urban countries in the world, and the London Basin is its epicenter.

This area of rolling scarps and valleys around the River Thames was once the most important region in the world. Originally an Imperial Roman outpost, by the end of the eighteenth century London had become the first city since Rome itself to reach a population of one million. As you approach London, you approach the Greenwich Meridian: the zero line on the maps everyone— including the pilot of your aircraft—uses to navigate the planet. This is one of the many tangible holdovers of the days when London was capital to a global empire; the widespread usage of the English language is another.

In Ireland, fast-growing and newly prosperous Dublin is experiencing sprawl similar to London's, but here the concentration of population in the capital region is even more pronounced. One in three people in Ireland lives in the Dublin area, and the rest of the island is very sparsely populated, with no other large cities. Instead, Ireland is characterized by rock-strewn, rolling hills and pasture dotted with tiny villages and towns. As is apparent from the air, much of Ireland is relatively undeveloped, and on the ground it can have a desolate feeling—

besides Iceland, Ireland is the least forested country in Europe. But unlike Iceland, Ireland's barrenness is the result of human agency: The Emerald Isle was once covered in thick woods, now long gone to clearing and grazing.

You'll notice that, like other large cities, London and Dublin draw in transportation links. Railroads, highways, roads, canals, even the Thames itself (although of course it was there first) head into the hub of London like spokes on a wheel. It's quite likely that you're heading there, too: Heathrow, London's primary airport, serves more international passengers than any other in the world. Sixty-three million people fly through here each year—three million more than live in the United Kingdom. Together with Gatwick and Stanstead airports, this makes London the biggest air travel hub in the world, serving 110 million people annually.

Of course, it's always possible that you won't see any of this because of overcast weather. Great Britain and Ireland are notorious for their gray skies and steady rainfall, particularly in the winter. All this moisture means farmers rarely need to irrigate here, which has allowed the development of many small farms scattered about the countryside—the agricultural pattern you see beneath you would simply not be possible in a drier region, where farmland would be clustered around water sources like rivers, lakes, canals, or wells.

While rain and fog afflicts the western portions of the British Isles most consistently, you may notice that London is grayer than the rest of its environs. Indeed, it was here that the word "smog" was coined in the nineteenth century to connote the ubiquitous (at that time) miasma that was considered a beautiful side effect of technological progress. While London has been far cleaner since coal burning in the city was banned after a killer smog in 1952, the urban heat and pollution emanating from the city still affect the weather here (see Smog, page 168).

The eastern coast of England differs greatly from the rugged west. Here, the land is lower and flatter, with heavy human intervention along the coastline. The most dramatic is in the Fens, an area of flat, rich farmland that was reclaimed from marshland along the North Sea. Look for a very flat area with sharply defined fields and long, straight canals on the coast north of East Anglia. It's no accident that the landscape here, with its dikes, windmills, and flat farmland, is reminiscent of the Low Countries: Dutch engineers helped in the large-scale draining of the marshes two centuries ago. At the southern end of this coastline, where the British Isles come closest to continental Europe at the Strait of Dover, see if you can spot the massive new road and rail interchange that is the British landfall of the Channel Tunnel, the undersea rail link that at long last ended Britain's insularity and made it indisputably a part of Europe (see Transportation, page 41). Near here, too, you may spot the famous white cliffs of Dover—towering walls of chalk that gave ancient Britain its Latin name: Albion.

The campus landscape—a collection of buildings arranged in a parklike setting—dates back to the thirteenth century, when Oxford University first established its system of residential colleges. This versatile layout—one that allows expansion while maintaining coherence—became the model for many of the oldest universities around the world (just as the curriculum and didactic methods at Oxford have also inspired widespread imitation). In operation for at least nine hundred years (the exact date of its founding is lost in the mists of time), Oxford is the oldest English-language university.

The Oxford campus is like a city within a city, providing services for a population of more than 25,000 staff and students. (Some campuses are far bigger still: Europe's largest university, La Sapienza, in Rome, has 180,000 students.) Courtyards and sweeping networks of pedestrian walkways between buildings are telltale signs of campuses. Unlike many modern public spaces, campuses are explicitly—and from the air, visibly—designed for walking.

The campus layout has been adopted by many different kinds of institutions that must integrate a wide variety of activities, from office work to recreation to dining, in a small area outside—or even within—the density of an urban setting.

The word "campus" comes to us from the Latin for "field," a feature that can be seen clearly at the Saarland University Campus, shown here.

Besides universities and corporate campuses, other examples of institutional landscape design you are likely to see on your flight include prisons, hospitals, and military bases. Each sort has its own distinctive characteristics, with the features of prisons being perhaps the most extreme:

SAARLAND UNIVERSITY: Founded by the French government in occupied Germany in 1948, Saarland University was the first of the postwar generation of European universities. Its physical layout reflects the much older university campus tradition that dates back more than a thousand years: it is human-scaled, and conducive to walking, with plenty of paths and little parking. Buildings and open spaces for different uses are intermingled with one another. Different sections of the campus are self-contained, yet interconnected enough with other parts to create a coherent public space that engenders informal, personal interactions among its more than 15,000 students.

Watch for perimeters clear of buildings and shrubbery, fences (often double), and architecture designed to permit clear views by guards (sharp angles, H-shaped buildings, and other configurations). At night, prisons are brightly illuminated and, because they are often in rural areas, they can be seen very easily. Military bases often appear as sprawling assemblages of distinctively repeating buildings and warehouses, often centered on a runway.

AIRBUS HEADQUARTERS: Airbus, the leading airliner manufacturer and pillar of European industry, maintains this corporate campus and assembly plant in Blagnac, next to the Airport serving Tolouse, France. While the research campus was a natural consequence of the establishment of private research institutions modeled on universities, the siting of corporate head offices in campus settings is a later American innovation. Management once depended on the physical proximity to a community of peers and services like banking that city centers afford, but modern communications have allowed other considerations to come to the fore—most notably land prices and quality of life for office workers. In 2002, the largest corporate campus in the world—160 ha or 400 acres—was built outside Madrid by Santander Central Hispano, the biggest bank in the euro zone. Unlike most older universities, corporate campuses are outside the main part of cities, lack major sports facilities, and are without residential space: look for vast parking lots instead.

FRANCE

		GEOLOGICAL FEATURES		
	River Basins	Alps	Uplands	Escarpments

			HYDROLOGICAL FEATURES	
			Rivers	Coastlines

			ECOLOGICAL FEATURES	
			Forests	Marshes

		HUMAN FEATURES		
		Railroads	Farms	Compact Rural Towns

BONUS SIGHTS
Paris, ancient volcanoes, endless vineyards, cute villages, signs of old wars

France epitomizes a fusion of ancient tradition with advanced modernity like few other places on Earth. Since the year 843 CE France has held to more or less the same borders as today, making it one of the world's oldest states. The country has long been self-sufficient and self-contained, in many ways a world unto itself. Yet at the same time, France is cosmopolitan and has an outward-looking tradition. Both the nation's global colonial history and the interconnectedness its geography affords with its neighbors set the stage for France's prominent profile in the modern world.

As you'll see from the air, France is naturally isolated enough to be a coherent territory, yet the barriers—the Pyrenees to the south, the Alps to the southeast and especially the Rhine and the Low Countries to the northeast—are porous enough to encourage robust connections with neighboring countries. Historically, of course, these "robust connections" have meant not only trade and cultural exchange, but also invasions by and of various neighbors. Yet France has always eventually returned to roughly the same footprint once hostilities have ended.

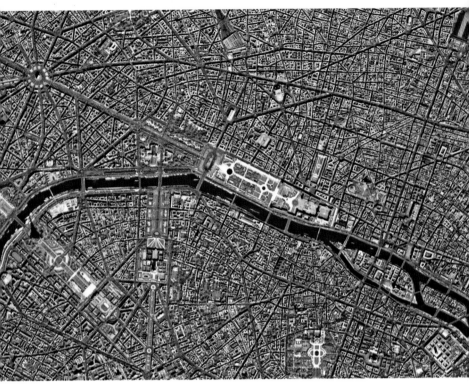

PARIS: The Parisian layout has been repeated around the world so often that it has become the archetype of the grand imperial city. But as much as the city's distinctive look is the result of aggressive redevelopment in the nineteenth century, it is also a monument to the restraint shown by Parisian authorities in subsequent decades. Rather than foster a core of postwar high-rise office buildings, planners here consciously retained the close, low profile of the city center. The result is an urban area unlike any other.

The land itself is a collection of coastal plains, basins, valleys, and uplands that define distinctive regions. The northern coast, which includes Normandy and Brittany, is a wild and remote region of rocky headlands and secluded beaches. Watch for clusters of slate-roofed houses in villages along the coast and in the rolling farmland inland. In contrast, the Rhine valley is more heavily settled and, unsurprisingly, is reminiscent of adjacent areas in Germany.

The Paris Basin reigns as the most important region of France. Geographically, it is a broad area of low-lying land surrounded by ranks of arching escarpments (watch for these long ridges especially if you're flying west out of Paris). The sedimentary rock here is the remains of an ancient shallow seabed more than 2 kilometers (1 mi.) thick. The escarpments are the edges of different rock layers that have been pushed upward—warped by the same forces that gave rise to the Alps farther south (see Plate Tectonics, page 102). The flat and rolling landscape you see today was created by the action of erosion over the eons.

The Seine River is the main drainage from the Paris Basin. On an island in the middle of this river, at the intersection of an important ancient overland trading route with the Seine, the Celts founded the City of Paris long before the Roman arrival two thousand years ago. In the following centuries, the city grew beyond the original Île de la Cité (at the bottom right of the image on the facing page) to encompass both banks of the Seine as well, and to become the center of French culture, as it has remained for nearly a millennium and a half.

This growth—today there are 11.5 million inhabitants in greater Paris—obliterated many of the ancient settlements. Still, some historical elements are visible from the air. Paris' five concentric sets of defensive walls chronicle the city's growth like the rings of a tree (and unintentionally echo the ringed escarpments around the Paris Basin). For the most part, however, today's view from above Paris is dominated by features from the last two centuries of this great city's history.

The straight, broad boulevards that you can see running through central Paris were created by Baron Georges Eugène Haussmann in the 1850s as part of a modernization of the city that also included new sewers and water supplies, railway stations, public parks and monuments, and bridges. The majestic vistas afforded by this layout became the defining characteristic of city planning in that century, and the model was imitated around the world. The boulevards also made it easier for central authorities to manage the city's dense urban neighborhoods, called *arrondissements*, and the uprisings that frequently broke out during the turbulent nineteenth century.

That century closed with the Belle Epoque, when many of Paris' most famous—and visible—monuments were created. If you're flying by, look for the iconic Eiffel Tower, built for the Exposition Universelle of 1889. The tallest structure on Earth for forty years (look for its distinctive shape on the southern side of the Seine a little to the west of the central part of the city, toward the left in the image on the facing page), the Eiffel Tower endures as the quintessential symbol of Paris' embrace of both past and future. If you've got sharp eyes and know where to look, you might also be able to spot other famous sites like the Arc de Triomphe (at the top left of the image), Versailles, the Bois de Boulogne, and more.

As you fly above Paris you'll notice that the city is heavily populated, yet relatively free of modern sprawl. Paris' density is unusual in Europe. After World War II, when many urbanites left Western centers like London and most American cities in favor of growing suburbs, Paris retained a tightly integrated mix of urban housing and businesses that contributes to its distinctive feel and compact, mosaic-like look from above. Instead of permitting the growth of a downtown core of skyscrapers, Parisian authorities in the postwar period consciously maintained the character of their city by forcing that sort of development into a new center—La Défense, the concentration of tall buildings to the west of the city center you'll easily spot from the air. Here you may be able to pick out the Grande Arche, its clean lines a modernist nod to the more ornate Arc de Triomphe, and the western terminus of the Axe Historique, a line of monuments and plazas that stretches from old center to new.

Also during this period—primarily the 1960s onward—the construction of public housing projects in the *banlieues* (suburbs) of Paris created the landscape you'll see outside the urban center. A postwar building boom brought modernist towers crammed with low-cost apartments to the areas surrounding Paris. This pattern of high-rise development on cheap land outside the urban core can be seen in the contemporary skyline of many cities around the world. Built of prefab concrete slabs and arranged in clusters around transportation corridors, housing like this is also found in Latin America, Asia, and the formerly Communist countries. In the late 1970s, this element of city planning, called *les grandes ensembles* in France, came to be seen less as modern and clean and more as monotonous and deadening, and fell from favor. The

CROP MARKS: Ghostly patterns in the fields around the town of Bordeaux-en-Gâtinais, in central France near the Loire River, reveal the locations of old—possibly ancient—roads, fields, and settlements. Some of these lines extend modern roads or boundaries, showing that these contemporary features have been in place for a long time. Others reveal long-gone settlements. Patterns like this are caused by variation in crop vigor as a result of underlying soil characteristics where different activities once took place. They can be seen only from the air, sometimes only during certain seasons or times of day, and their study has been an important archaeological advance in the past century. In this case, the general pattern of the vanished landscape is remarkably similar to the present-day scene, a testament to the French policy of preserving, through agricultural supports and import restrictions, a rural landscape of small towns set in clusters of irregular fields.

CHATEAUX: The famous French chateaux are most concentrated in the Loire valley. Status symbols of French nobility from the tenth century onward, chateaux range from little more than large houses to elaborate castles. From above, typical features include a symmetrical plan (often with a rectangular garden) set on wooded grounds that are also laid out symmetrically. This example, at Dampierre-en-Yvelines, is in a bucolic area southwest of Paris and is still owned by the family for which it was built three centuries ago. Similar country estates can be seen throughout Europe, remnants of the continent's long history of hereditary nobility.

program was abandoned in the 1980s in favor of new development in the city center. More recently, the focus has turned to the rehabilitation of these postwar blocks in an effort to make them more habitable, although this did not prevent them from incubating widespread social unrest in 2005.

As you fly above, you'll see that road and rail links head out from Paris in all directions, covering the country in a transportation network spreading outward from the capital city. To be sure, other French regional centers are important in their own right, but none comes close to Paris' influence.

Flying south of Paris, you'll see the land rises into the undulating hills and small mountains of the Massif Central, which lies in the center of southern France. These hills are centered on a cluster of old volcanoes, which accounts for the many hot springs in the region. Though you won't be able to spot any springs from the air, see if you can pick out conical volcanic forms and ancient calderas (craters formed by volcanic eruptions).

VINEYARDS: Vineyards in the Rhône Valley, one of France's famous wine regions, are easily identified by their telltale rows of green. In the fall, they turn bright yellow and red, and in the winter the vines remain as brown lines across the fields. Except for the highway, the landscape here has changed little for millennia—this was a major wine-producing region even in the time of the Roman Empire. The characteristic rows of trees along the fields serve to protect the vines from wind. For hundreds of years, French wine has been carefully classified by the area in which it was produced. For the past hundred years, it has been illegal to make false claims about the origins of traditional products like wine, cheese, and butter. While cumbersome, this system of appellation has ensured that French wine has remained the standard against which all others are measured.

Most of the population in southern France lives in the lowlands of Bordeaux in the west and the Rhône Valley in the east, as well as along the Mediterranean coast. The Massif Central serves as a rugged barrier that has historically kept these centers separate from one another, though not so impenetrably as to be isolated. As you fly over southern France you'll see the Massif Central itself is largely rolling pastureland with a few major towns, while the surrounding lowlands are more heavily settled with dense networks of farming towns and industrial cities.

The French cherish this patchwork of irregularly shaped farms separated by hedgerows and interspersed with tiny farm towns. They see in this landscape the continuance of traditional French agricultural strength and diversity. Nevertheless, this bucolic countryside is maintained only at a price: subsidies and regulations help to provide markets for the crops that are grown here in spite of cheaper options from abroad.

THE SUBURBAN JUNGLE: While downtown Paris is the charming epitome of the worldly city, the area to its southeast is what makes it work. This jumble of infrastructure, which includes Orly airport and a nearby prison, the huge railway switching yards and sewage treatment plants seen here, and huge cemeteries that from the air can look uncannily and disturbingly like parking lots, makes it possible to have so many people living so closely together. This scale of organization marked a new level in human development beginning in the nineteenth century (previously only ancient Rome had come close), and though it may not be the prettiest landscape, it is essential to the operation of the global economy and culture. Note the parks here made from former gravel pits in the Seine floodplain: The genius of energetic development is that it can usually find a way to turn all but the worst messes into some kind of silver lining. Also note the small residential area surrounded by the switching yard, sewage treatment plant, and highways. This sort of neglect is a sure sign that this is a neighborhood of politically powerless poor people.

Across France you'll notice some regional variation in the rural landscapes. Farm size is related both to local soil and climatic conditions and to the value of the crop—where crops with lower returns thrive, they must be grown for profitability on large farms, which can be worked more efficiently. In the Paris Basin, larger farms grow wheat, while in much of the rest of the country medium-sized plots produce a variety of staples. High-value, labor-intensive crops like wine grapes and flowers can support the smallest farms, as you'll see in wine-producing regions like the Rhône Valley. Look for lines of vines traversing hillsides; in the fall they'll be bright yellow or red. In the summer, watch for bright yellow fields of sunflowers, a classic feature of the French countryside.

The pattern of small—often tiny—rural towns is also typically French. Though you'll see similar landscapes elsewhere, in France this preindustrial settlement style has been consciously preserved as much as possible in the high-tech present. Historically, each town provided the surrounding farms and rural dwellers with the services they needed, which to some extent they still do. Nonetheless, France, like all of Europe, has seen a rural exodus due to urbanization and mechanization.

In the Middle Ages, in areas prone to conflict, people built walled cities called *bastides*. In a departure from the feudal practice prevailing at the time, whereby peasant farmers were taxed by local lords, *bastides* were created in order to establish safe control points for trade and thus specifically to tax merchants rather than farmers. Watch for towns with a grid layout within walls and a partly covered central marketplace, very picturesque reminders of the ancient society here.

Today France's rural towns remain an important part of the nation's political fabric. The nearly forty thousand mayors in the country have an important voice in the nation's internal affairs, and are a strong constituency for policies that promote the traditional rural landscape.

Farther south, France's Mediterranean coast has a somewhat different focus from the rest of the nation. Its affinities have historically been toward other Mediterranean countries: The ancient Phoenicians founded Marseille, for example, and today that city is strongly influenced by France's former North African colonies. As in neighboring Spain and Italy, the coast is a major tourist draw, and development here has been ferocious in the past few decades. If you fly along the Côte d'Azur, for example, you'll see massive tourist development in the form of high-rise hotels, golf courses, marinas, and other leisure infrastructure crowded along the coast.

Corsica, France's largest Mediterranean island, is separated from the country's mainland by more than just water. The landscape here is different, of the sort found throughout the rugged islands and peninsulas washed by the Mediterranean; Maquis, a thicketlike dry forest, covers most of the island's middle elevations. Likewise, Corsica's culture and language have long been proudly distinct, making its relationship to the rest of France often turbulent. Like similarly distinctive regions in other countries (the Basque Country, Scotland, Lappland, Sardinia, and elsewhere), Corsica is forging a new, more independent identity in the political space afforded by European unification.

Transportation networks blanket Europe, as you can't help but notice from the air—after all, your vantage point is part of one such network. The airports, planes, and invisible but sharply demarcated high-altitude jetways all make up the air transportation network that carries thirty thousand flights or more each day. Nine million commercial flights each year take place in the Eurocontrol area (the air traffic control zone that includes all of Europe except Russia).

But looking back down, on the ground is where you'll spot the more visible—and more heavily traveled—transportation networks. Roadways and canals have carried people and goods throughout Europe since time immemorial, and railways have helped define modern Europe.

Together, these networks serve to unite regions and countries—and Europe as a whole—by facilitating the movement of goods and people. Historically, these routes have also spread ideas, cultures, and languages, as well more deleterious consequences of connectivity, like disease and conflict.

Transportation networks are full-scale maps of economic activity. When you see a region densely furnished with roadways and train tracks, you can assume the area is wealthy (see Wealth, page 126). Cities with many links radiating outward are centers that economically dominate their regions. Within large networks, you'll be able to see smaller networks repeating similar patterns.

Paved roads, as opposed to dirt paths for people and animals, have existed in Europe continuously since at least the time of the Roman Empire. Roman roads served as the main long-distance overland routes in

(continued)

300 ft, 100 m

THE CHANNEL TUNNEL: This massive transportation nexus is the British end of the Channel Tunnel, the 50 kilometer (31 mi.) set of railway tunnels that connect England and France beneath the English Channel. Cars and trucks are driven onto specially designed trains, which then disappear into the hole at right for the 35-minute crossing. The Chunnel is emblematic of the new, more unified Europe for it breaches a barrier that has traditionally kept England apart from affairs on the Continent. The project also highlights the scale of the European effort: It was launched in the 1970s, and construction took seven years (the Chunnel opened in 1994 and cost almost 15 billion euros). Note the chalk horse on the grassy slope above the facility. Completed in 2003 of chalk slabs, this is part of a regional artistic tradition dating back to the Iron Age in which turf is removed to reveal the white chalk substrate.

Europe for centuries before they were supplanted by railways in the 1800s. Many of the original roads—including the first Roman Road, the Via Appia (the Appian Way) in Italy, built in 312 BCE—are still major routes today. In some cases the actual roadbeds are still in use.

More recently, the German system of autobahns became the model for the development of divided highways around the world. Developed in the 1930s to connect major centers and, not incidentally, to speed the movement of military personnel and equipment, the system impressed the invading American general Dwight Eisenhower so much that, as president a few years later, he modeled America's great interstate system after it. From the air, look for the telltale double lines of roadway, as well as looping interchanges.

You'll also notice train tracks across the land. Europe is the native land of the train. The first successful railroad was built in northern England, in the 1820s. Very quickly, steam locomotives became the fire-breathing symbols of the Industrial Revolution, and countless miles of track were laid around the world in a few decades. (By 1851 India had its first

(continued)

AUTOBAHN: The first superhighway connected Milan and Venice, but it was in Germany that the idea blossomed. Here, an interchange on the outskirts of Berlin displays many features invented in Germany: Looping on and off ramps allow entry and exit without slowing down; traffic in different directions is separated; banked curves and wide lanes accommodate high speeds; and bridged intersections allow roads to cross without stopping traffic. Also note the train tracks leading into the heart of the city; the three overlapping gray rectangles are a commuter train station. Road and rail are connected in a spaghetti-like dance, forming a larger transportation system that your plane is a part of, too.

railroad, for example.) Europe continues to be among the world leaders in train traffic, with modern high-speed links heading in all directions. From on high, watch for single or double strands of track, usually on broad rights-of-way carved through the countryside. Also watch for switching yards, where you'll see the roadbed expand into dozens of parallel tracks. In cities, look for these in combination with the telltale arching roofs of railway stations. Big stations often identify nineteenth-century urban centers.

In addition to autobahns and railroad tracks, keep your eyes open for heavily trafficked waterways. Europe's rivers and canals are of huge economic importance. With its basins and plains and its large, slow rivers, Europe is well suited to canal-building. Look for long straight waterways, often interrupted by locks and limned with roadways or paths.

Canals typically string together natural bodies of water, such as rivers and lakes, to enable very long distance water transport. The Rhine, for example, has more than 800 kilometers (about 500 mi.) of navigable waterways and carries hundreds of millions of tons of freight each year, making it the busiest inland waterway in Europe—watch for the rectangular barges making their way up and down the river.

The Rhine-Main-Danube canal in central Germany, as well as locks at choke points like Romania's Iron Gate, make it possible to travel by water all the way from the Black Sea to the North Sea.

CHARLES DE GAULLE AIRPORT: Paris' Charles de Gaulle Airport is Europe's second busiest. Notwithstanding architectural flourishes in the terminals, an airport is all business. It's about moving as many planes as possible in and out of the air (in this case more than half a million each year), and as many people as possible (200,000 per day) from air to road and rail and vice versa. Although one man has been living in Terminal One—at the center of the blossom of jets—for more than ten years, this isn't a place to linger. From above it is clear that the design is purely for the convenience of cars and planes.

Most newer airports are in the countryside where they can sprawl: The new superjumbo Airbus A380 requires runways of nearly 4,000 meters (two and a half miles). And low-flying jets are more than an annoyance: The noise affects nearby residents' physical and mental health.

THE NORTH

THE LOW COUNTRIES
THE NORDIC COUNTRIES
ICELAND

ICELAND

Reykjavik

Norwegian
Sea

FINLAND

SWEDEN

Helsinki

THE NORDIC COUNTRIES

NORWAY

Oslo

Stockholm

Baltic Sea

North
Sea

DENMARK
Copenhagen

Malmö

THE LOW COUNTRIES

Amsterdam

NETHERLANDS

Rotterdam

RUHR RIVER

BELGIUM

Brussels

RHINE RIVER

THE NORTH

THE LOW COUNTRIES

GEOLOGICAL FEATURES

Sand Dunes	Moraines	River Delta	Barrier Islands

HYDROLOGICAL FEATURES

River Delta	Estuaries	Lagoons	Lakes	Marshes

ECOLOGICAL FEATURES

Marshes	Estuaries	Wooded Uplands

HUMAN FEATURES

Canals	Dikes	Dams	Polders	Cities

BONUS SIGHTS
Amsterdam's canals, the Frisian Islands, Luxembourg

Few places on Earth have been as thoroughly adapted for human habitability as the Low Countries, which comprise Belgium and the Netherlands. Except for Wallonia—the southern, French-speaking part of Belgium, which is forested upland—the Low Countries are a region of flat marshes and sandy glacial moraines around the delta where the Rhine, Mass, and Scheldt rivers meander into the sea (see Glacial Terrain, page 60). But centuries of draining the land and erecting barriers against encroaching seas have created a hospitable and unique landscape. The Dutch part of the region especially has been so modified that from the air it's difficult to spot many natural features at all. Instead, you'll see spread out below you the magnificent engineering project that is the Netherlands.

The landscape is a carefully maintained, artificial realm of canals and polders—land reclaimed from the sea or coastal lakes and marshes. Look for the telltale angular signs of the human hand: perfectly rectangular, flat fields; long, straight shorelines and watercourses; and berms (raised earthworks that contain

POLDER: The town of Zoeterwoude sits in a classic polder—land that has been reclaimed from the sea. Polders are enclosed by dikes (earthen walls that prevent flooding) and kept dry with pumps (formerly powered by the famous Dutch windmills). Because the land itself came about as an act of planning, the roads, canals, boundaries, and other features of a polder are all carefully ordered and maintained. Similar areas of flat, rich farmland can be seen in other parts of Europe, including the Fens in England, the Frisian coast in Germany, and even in central Italy where Apennine lakes have been drained.

watercourses) and dams. These modifications began fifteen hundred years ago, as Scandinavians settled in the Rhine delta and built hundreds of earthen mounds upon which they lived in small villages, out of reach of floods and tides. By the ninth century, dikes came into use. Earthen ramparts that protect enclosed areas from flooding, the dikes made the development of the region possible. By the seventeenth century, dikes and windmills (to pump out water) came to define the Dutch countryside—a landscape that inspired the saying, "God made the world, but the Dutch made the Netherlands."

Today, you'll see from the air a sophisticated system of earthen dikes, flat polders, canals, pumping stations, and sluice dams (partial barriers that allow some water flow) in a completely managed land- and waterscape. Nearly half of the Netherlands lies below sea level ("nether" means low), and the Dutch have always been acutely aware of this precarious situation—floods from both river and sea have killed thousands in the past.

Out of necessity, the Dutch have become masters of environmental planning and coordination—polders do not happen by accident, but are the result of careful design and cooperation, followed by diligent maintenance. Indeed, the boards that govern local water management date back to the twelfth century and are some of the oldest extant democratic bodies in the world.

And the effort is ongoing: The Deltaworks, a massive project of dams, canals, and sea barriers at the mouths of the Rhine-Maas delta in the southern part of the Netherlands, was completed in 2002 after five decades of work. Called one of the greatest engineering marvels ever attempted, many of its details are visible from your window: Watch for long, low berms and causeways punctuated by blocky structures (these are gates to prevent flooding while still allowing routine circulation) stretching across wide expanses of water.

But there's more work to do: The Netherlands' unique geography and land management has led to keen environmental awareness—as sea levels rise with global warming, for example, the Netherlands is likely to be among the most heavily impacted European nations.

The Dutch way of meticulous management encompasses the entire country. If you're flying in this region, you'll probably be landing at Schiphol, the Netherlands' primary airport—the runways of which are 5 meters (15 ft.) below sea level. When you're in the air near Schiphol, you'll be inside Randstad Holland—the Ring City that comprises Amsterdam, Utrecht, Rotterdam, the Hague, Haarlem, and other cities in an urban donut of seven million people around a core of bucolic farmland. While located just southwest of Amsterdam, Schiphol serves all of Randstad Holland, the rural center of which is strictly zoned to prevent unwanted suburbanization of the country.

The Dutch are determined to preserve a landscape that includes very intensive agriculture in the midst of one of the most densely populated regions on Earth. The Netherlands remains among the largest exporters of agricultural products in the world. In springtime watch for the bright colors of the famous tulip bulb fields near Haarlem as well as the long, white structures that are extensive greenhouses producing everything from grapes to flowers to herbs—a tradition that dates back more than a century. Greenhouses cover just 5 percent of Dutch agricultural land, yet yield a fifth of the value of the nation's harvest.

Your visit to Schiphol is an affirmation of the Low Countries' growth into a transportation hub for all of Europe. Ever since the fifteenth century, when

The most immediately visible feature of water management on the landscape is the reservoir formed behind a dam. Watch for long, branched bodies of water with one conspicuously flat end—that's the dam. You're most likely to spot these in mountainous areas, where the land forms narrow-mouthed natural basins that lend themselves to dam building. In less hilly areas, like Ukraine's steppes (see page 144), dams create reservoirs that can stretch for hundreds of kilometers. The water surface of a reservoir is flat, so the relative jaggedness or smoothness of the shoreline is an indication of how rugged the terrain around the dammed river course is.

Dams and the reservoirs behind them provide water, flood control, aquatic recreation, and in many cases, hydroelectric power, although they also disrupt river ecosystems.

You are also likely to see canals during your flight. These long, narrow channels are used for navigation and water distribution, and are often connected to natural bodies of water. You'll see thousands of kilometers of navigable canals throughout Europe, where many have been in use for thousands of years.

Irrigation by other means, including flooding and the use of wells, shows up as lush green crop areas in landscapes that are otherwise drier and browner. In southern Europe in particular, irrigation is the key to habitability. In very dry areas, watch for pivot irrigation: circular fields of green fed from a well at the center by a wheeled pipe festooned with sprinklers moving like the arm of an old-fashioned radar screen.

Sewage-treatment plants are also important components of water systems. The sewage treatment plant at right in Saint Petersburg's harbor helps reduce the substantial pollution the city of five million releases into the Baltic Sea. The different rectangular and circular tanks are where incoming sewage is settled, separated into liquid and solid components, aerated, and biologically degraded. Though unglamorous, plants like this—you'll see them along water-courses near any developed city or town—are indispensable interfaces between the human and natural worlds. Not only do they help keep the environment clean, but they are critical to stopping the spread of disease in the dense cities we humans favor: Diseases like cholera and typhoid were once serious problems throughout Europe.

EUROPORT

KIEL CANAL: Connecting the Elbe estuary and the North Sea to the Baltic, the 100 kilometer (62 mi.) long Kiel Canal lets oceangoing ships bypass the long and dangerous journey through the Skaw, the waterway between Denmark and Sweden. Serving more than 100 ships each day, the Kiel Canal is the busiest artificial waterway in the world, the modern (opened in 1895 and enlarged thereafter) version of a canal first built in the eighteenth century.

Amsterdam broke the Hanseatic League's monopoly on Baltic trade, the region has been at the nexus of Europe's strongest centers—Paris to the south, England to the west, Scandinavia to the north, and the Ruhr and Rhineland to the east.

With modern containerization (the practice of packing goods in metal boxes that can be loaded on ships, trains, and trucks alike—look for these brightly colored containers stacked around ports) and the increase in global trade, the region's natural advantage has become even more pronounced. Europoort, a massive postwar coastal port extension, makes Rotterdam the largest port in Europe and one of the largest in the world. Belgium's port of Antwerp, just to the south and sharing many of the same advantages, is Europe's second largest. These and other ports are easily spotted from the air: Look for blocky, branched waterways surrounded by cranes, warehouses, and mountains of stacked containers.

CONTAINER PORT: From Rotterdam to the sea, a massive complex that includes the huge Europoort development is the biggest port in Europe, and one of the largest in the world. As befits Dutch trading history, most of the cargo that passes through this port neither originates in nor is destined for the Netherlands. Indeed, a third of the trade through Rotterdam is German, transshipped via road, rail, canal, and pipeline (note the large oil terminal next to the Nieuwe Maas River, with its farm of white tanks). Industry here can easily access raw materials from all over the world and ship finished products anywhere, so the area around the port is thick with factories. Ninety percent of the world's cargo is containerized—note the piles of colorful containers on many of the wharves, as well as the gargantuan cranes for handling them and the laden container ship pulling into the main channel. This late twentieth century innovation has revolutionized world trade by greatly reducing transportation costs.

This hubbub of trade is further harnessed in the Low Countries by extensive value-added industries that depend on the flow of goods through the region. Look near the ports for assembly and processing plants (including oil refineries, distinguished by rows of cylindrical tanks, flares, and intricate tangles of pipe) where materials and parts from all over the world are put together or otherwise processed, then repackaged for shipment elsewhere.

As you fly south, the Low Countries afford a study in contrast between careful and haphazard planning. Flying from the Netherlands into Belgium, you'll see that the human-made elements of the landscape become disorderly. As far back as the fourteenth century, the growing city of Amsterdam undertook careful consideration of how it should enlarge, and to what purpose. Because growth meant draining and developing blocks of canals and large tracts of land all at once, the projects had to be centralized and carefully directed. Belgium's historical development, on the other hand, was less coordinated, depending more on localized economic activity. As a result, the landscape today is one of sprawl, in particular on the flatlands of Flanders.

If you get a chance to fly over both Amsterdam and Brussels, you'll see a clear illustration of divergent schools of urban planning. Brussels is developing along a more American model, with a city center of businesses surrounded by bedroom communities, while Amsterdam retains a lively mix contained within a sharply defined urban area that changes abruptly into farmland at the city's edge.

THE NORDIC COUNTRIES

			GEOLOGICAL FEATURES		
		Old, Stony Mountain Ranges	Fjords	Coastal Plains

			HYDROLOGICAL FEATURES		
		Fjords	Lakes	Glaciers

			ECOLOGICAL FEATURES		
				Boreal Forest

			HUMAN FEATURES		
		Farms	Fish Pens	Clearcuts

BONUS SIGHTS
Oslo's snug harbor, North Cape, Lapp villages, the Åland Islands, the Faroes

Europe's rugged north is a wild and lightly populated region that comprises Scandinavia—Norway, Sweden, and Denmark—plus the island nation of Iceland, which was colonized by Scandinavian peoples, and Finland, which, while part of the same geographical region, is culturally distinct. For most of its history, this area has seen much less human impact than its neighbors to the south.

The Fennoscandian Peninsula—Scandinavia plus Finland and Karelia in Russia—juts to the north and west from Eurasia and encloses the Baltic Sea, a shallow depression formed by a great ice cap during the last ice age. Since the ice melted, Earth's surface has been free to rebound, a process that continues today: Each year the land rises by up to a centimeter, exposing more and more territory around the sea's edges, particularly in the north.

You'll see the mark of ice everywhere in the Nordic countries (see Glacial Terrain, page 60). And while regions farther south in Europe also show evidence of past glaciation, in northern Scandinavia the ice is still present—you'll see permanent ice caps year-round in the Scandinavian mountains. Two billion years old, the rock here is the most ancient in Europe and has been scoured again and again by glaciers. You'll see from the air many areas of smoothly rounded, exposed rock.

The rugged Scandinavian mountains are part of an ancient range that stretches into the British Isles. Their spine extends along the border between Norway and Sweden from southern Norway all the way to the country's North Cape, the most northerly point in Europe. Largely treeless, the flanks of these mountains are covered in high pasture and, toward the north, frozen tundra. Because this region is so remote, you'll fly over it only on certain routes, such as from the British Isles to Japan or other Far Eastern destinations.

Compared to other regions of the globe at similar latitudes, the Nordic countries are reasonably habitable. The North Atlantic Drift, the current that brings warm water all the way from the Gulf of Mexico, ensures that even as far north as Norway's Lofoten Islands, north of the Arctic Circle, winter temperatures often stay above freezing. But make no mistake—it does get cold here. On a winter visit, you'll find most of the region under a blanket of brilliantly white snow. If you fly here during the summer months, you'll see that much of Scandinavia is quite green.

The relative warmth has made it possible for the region to nurture a highly developed culture and to build an advanced economy not seen anywhere else at these latitudes. Though it is the least populated part of Europe, Scandinavia is one of the wealthiest regions in the world, with globally recognized companies like Nokia, Volvo, and Ikea originating here. From above, this wealth manifests itself as neatly developed, well-maintained infrastructure; plenty of cars and lights; and an extensive power grid (see Wealth, page 126). Much of the power here is hydroelectric—you'll easily spot the many dams and reservoirs in the region, particularly in the Scandinavian mountains.

The lowlands in the south—particularly the Danish island of Zealand and the adjacent Swedish region of Skåne—form the cultural center of Scandinavia. The nearby cities of Copenhagen and Malmö anchor this vibrant and growing region. The fertile plains here, left behind as the land rebounded following glaciation, combined with the long summer days—in June, the sun sets as late as 10 P.M. in Copenhagen—make this the most agriculturally productive part of the Nordic countries. Denmark especially, with its rolling moraines (see Glacial Terrain, page 60), is the region's agricultural heartland. Flying over the area, you'll see copious rolling farmland bearing typical northern crops such as potatoes, oats, wheat, and rye, or given over to animal husbandry (principally dairy, poultry, and swine).

You'll also see tiny pockets of agriculture elsewhere, including far up Norway's coastal fjords—deep, flooded glacial valleys left behind where huge

SOGNE FJORD: At 203 kilometers (126 mi.), Sogne Fjord is the second longest in the world. It is over 1,220 meters (4,000 ft.) deep before it enters the sea (fjords are not at their deepest where they enter the sea because they feature an undersea terminal moraine). While Norway's coast is famous for fjords—indeed the very word is Norwegian—they occur wherever glaciers once flowed out of a mountain range into the sea, notably British Columbia and Alaska, New Zealand, Labrador, Greenland, and Chile. It's easy to see why these protected waterways have long been favored by fishing communities: Boats here are sheltered from the fury of the sea, yet still have access to marine fishing grounds. The same advantages have today made these important locations for fish farming.

glaciers once ran into the sea. But the land here is only marginally arable: This region, with its dramatic coastline, has instead fostered a vibrant seafaring culture; see if you can spot any of the hundreds of tiny fishing villages nestled among the fjords. Fishing remains a crucial part of the economy in Norway, and fish farming abounds along this coast—you have a good chance of spotting salmon pens, rows of rectangular frames floating in sheltered waters.

For most of the past 100,000 years, sheets of ice several kilometers thick—halfway to the height of your plane at cruising altitude—covered all of the Nordic and Baltic countries, most of the British Isles, and the Northern European Plain in Germany and Poland. The ice began to retreat from the southern reaches of this range about 18,000 years ago, though it remains to this day in parts of the north—the Jostedal Glacier in Norway is the largest ice sheet in Europe outside Iceland.

Glaciers form when snow persists through the summer and builds up. The snow is compacted to ice and takes on liquid characteristics, flowing in (glacially) slow motion across the landscape and carving the land into distinct features.

MOUNTAINOUS AREAS

Mountain ranges accumulate ice caps during periods of cool climate—indeed, most of the remaining glaciers are in mountainous areas. The topography of most ranges has been heavily influenced by this ice.

Cirques are bowl-like valleys surrounded by high, steep walls. A glacier once sat here (and might still—remnants lie in cirques as far south as the Pyrenees). Arêtes are sharp ridges between cirques.

U-shaped valleys are long and broad with high, steep sides. These valleys, often featuring streams running through them, were once the courses of flowing glaciers. Along the coast, these valleys may be flooded to form fjords.

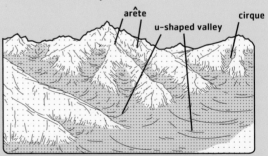

arête u-shaped valley cirque

mountainous areas

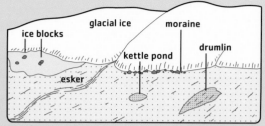

ice blocks · glacial ice · moraine · drumlin · kettle pond · esker

lowland areas

LOWLAND AREAS

The ice caps left plains of outwash—till (sand and gravel) deposited by meltwater—across the entire northern sector of Europe.

Moraines are high ridges of glacial till pushed up by the front and sides of moving glaciers or deposited at the foot of stationary ones. The size of moraines indicates the scale of the glaciers that created them—some of the largest are hundreds of miles long.

Eskers are sinuous ridges left by rivers that once flowed under ice sheets. Road surfaces are often located at their crests because of their convenient form.

Drumlins, also called whaleback hills, are distinguished by a high, rounded front and a long, tapering tail. Across a landscape, groups of drumlins all point in the same direction, parallel to the ancient glacier's motion.

Kettle ponds are round ponds or bogs created by melting chunks of ice left behind as a glacier receded.

Spillways are deep, wide valleys that once carried huge rivers of glacial meltwater. Many now have a much smaller river meandering across the bottom of the outsized valley.

The North Sea also brings Norway its greatest sources of modern wealth: oil and gas. The main Norwegian landfall for the undersea pipelines that run from the oil and gas platforms is Karstø, where you'll see an immense pipeline terminal on the coast—look for the large, well-lit coastal industrial facility that is part of the reason Norway is one of the largest oil and gas exporters in the world (see Energy, page 136).

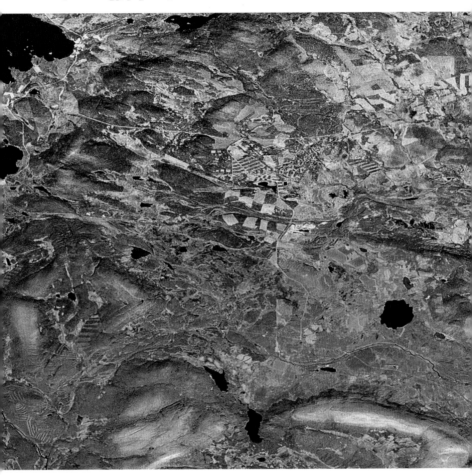

TAIGA: The taiga, or boreal forest, seen here in Lapland in northern Finland, is by far the biggest forest in Europe, and is part of the biggest in the world. It is an important source of wood for construction and manufacture, as well as for paper production. If you look closely as you fly here, you may be able to see the mills that make lumber, paper, or panels: They're large factories beside a body of water. Next to them are yards filled with logs and wood chips. This is also a mining region, and you may be able to spot piles of tailings and the tall smokestacks of smelters. In this image you can see a number of different styles of timber harvest, ranging from large block clearcuts to the less environmentally damaging innovation of strip cuts.

In contrast to the deep ocean off the Norwegian coast, the shallow Baltic Sea to the east of Scandinavia is calm and turbid, like a giant estuary. With many rivers feeding it and a narrow connection to the ocean, the Baltic is brackish—considerably less salty than the Atlantic. In the summer, look for green or reddish streaks or splotches in the water here. These cyanobacterial (algal) blooms are part of the natural Baltic ecosystem. But in recent years, agricultural runoff from the surrounding countries has caused the blooms to become overly dense, decreasing oxygen levels in the water and harming native fish. Because the countries surrounding the sea often have different priorities and resources, the Baltic region has historically been the stage for endless struggles. Today, this conflict is apparent in the poor coordination of responses to the declining health of the sea.

Dotted with picturesque and strategic islands, large parts of the Baltic Sea ice over in winter—look for expanses of flat white ice, often scored with narrow, dark channels created by icebreakers, specially reinforced ships that smash open shipping lanes like marine snowplows.

Inland, in low parts of Sweden and Finland surrounding the Baltic, you'll see flat or rolling land blanketed in forest. This is part of the boreal forest, or taiga, that covers the subarctic region around the globe. This characteristically cold, wet forest of conifers and a few hardy deciduous trees (principally birch here—look for their yellow leaves punctuating the landscape in early autumn) is the most northerly expanse of boreal woodlands in the world. An important source of timber for centuries, the forest here and in neighboring parts of Russia remains the primary European source of pulp for papermaking. Keep an eye out for large clearcuts, particularly in Finland, but note also how much of this forest is unbroken—the largest expanse in Europe by far.

Finland is also host to the most dramatic lakelands in Europe; looking from above, it's easy to believe the fact that water covers 10 percent of the country's area. North of Helsinki, the Lake Region, a granite basin scoured by glaciers to create countless bodies of water, is reminiscent of Northern Canada and is unique in all of Europe. It is justly celebrated by the Finns as one of their major tourist destinations.

As you move north, you'll see that the forestland thins out and eventually ceases. At this point you've reached the treeline. Once you've crossed the treeline you are in the High Arctic (see page 153).

ICELAND

Geographically, Iceland isn't part of any continent. This rugged island is new land born of an excrescence of magma from deep within Earth's crust (see Plate Tectonics, page 102). From 200 kilometers (125 mi.) beneath Iceland, a mantle plume—a hot upwelling in the magma—pushes liquid rock to the surface of the

FAULTLINES: Iceland's landscape may seem as though it's on another planet, but it's really just a particularly clear look at the processes that underlie much of Earth's surface. The faultlines here—long, straight seams in Earth's crust—mark places where the crust has been fractured by seismic activity. Watch too for volcanoes of various kinds, as well as very active glaciers.

water to create new land. All along the centerline of the Atlantic Ocean, two oceanic plates are being pulled apart, and the flow of magma into the breach has created the Mid-Atlantic Ridge. Thus Iceland, which continues to grow in this manner, marks the spreading zone between Europe and North America.

If Iceland seems like a land under construction, well, that's because it is. Its rough, stark beauty sings with pure geology: Volcanoes sputter and steam, and glaciers continue to carve the landscape (an eighth of the island is glaciated at present). If you get a chance to fly over Iceland, watch for the jumble of volcanoes and lava flows that cover the land, and look for steam from volcanic vents—Geysir, the eponymous geyser, is one of these. All this hot water is a happy benefit, providing clean geothermal heating and electricity to this self-reliant, remote nation.

Lying under 2.5 kilometers (1.5 mi.) of water in most places and stretching north-south the entire length of the Atlantic, the Mid-Atlantic Ridge is the longest mountain chain in the world, and the dark rocks you see in Iceland are

AFFLUENCE: In the Oslo suburb of Slependen, affluence graces the landscape. Large single-family houses nestle on wooded lots along the rocky, glacier-scoured ridges. Pleasure boats crowd the marinas in seemingly every neighborhood. Well-maintained highways whisk shoppers to the string of malls in the center of the image: The red-fronted building with plenty of parking in front of it is the local Ikea.

among the youngest on Earth. The Reykjanes Peninsula south and west of Reykjavík is part of this ridge, which stretches northeast across the island. From the air you'll see this directional trend clearly. Look for parallel ridges and fault lines—long, straight valleys or cracks that mark the edges between different chunks of crust.

With so much geological action going on here, it's no surprise that Iceland also includes some of the most active volcanoes in the world. There's always an eruption going on somewhere here, sometimes with dire consequences. In 1783, an eruption that decimated the island's livestock led to the starvation of a quarter of the nation's population.

The small island of Surtsey, just off Iceland's southern coast, sits at the center of the current geologic activity in the region. Indeed, Surtsey only emerged from the ocean in the 1960s, in an eruption of steam and fire that left behind a newly minted, if barren, Atlantic island.

THE MEDITERRANEAN

THE IBERIAN PENINSULA

ITALY

THE BALKAN PENINSULA

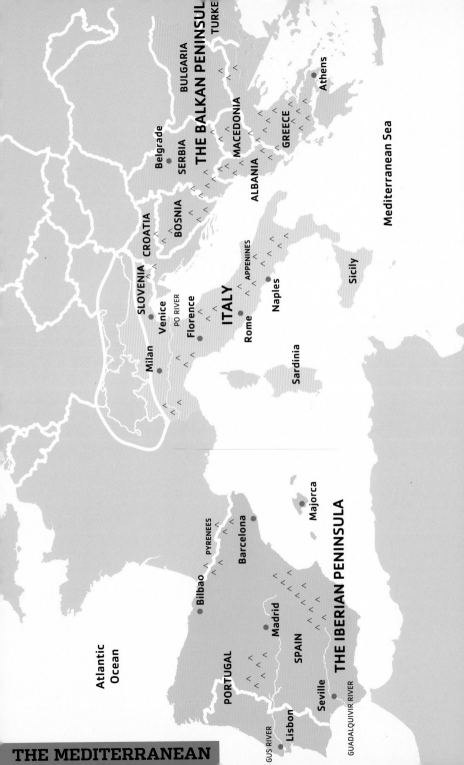

THE MEDITERRANEAN

THE IBERIAN PENINSULA

WATCH FOR

			GEOLOGICAL FEATURES	
			East-West Mountain Ranges ▲▲▲	Plateaus 🏛
			HYDROLOGICAL FEATURES	
		Rivers 〜	Reservoirs 〜	Rugged Coastlines ⌇
			ECOLOGICAL FEATURES	
			Mountain Pastures ⌓	Scrubland ѵѵѵѵѵ
			HUMAN FEATURES	
Reservoirs 〜	Irrigated Fields ⁞⁞⁞⁞⁞⁞	Towns 🏰	Tourist Development 📷	Ancient Cities Ⅲ

BONUS SIGHTS

Alhambra, the Sierra Nevada Mountains, Gibraltar and the Strait of Gibraltar, sprawling development

Like its own little subcontinent, the Iberian Peninsula juts squarishly seaward from Europe. From the air it looks almost like a land apart. Formed by a complex series of tectonic events, the peninsula, which comprises Portugal and Spain, tilts westward in a jumble of mountain ridges and plateaus (see Plate Tectonics, page 102).

Flying overhead, you'll see range after range, with five major sets of mountains and five major river valleys setting the stage for the region's complex history. For the most part, the rivers and ridges have an east-west orientation.

You'll notice, too, that the climate is graded in a series of different types. Situated between temperate Europe and the hot, dry lands of North Africa, and between the cool Atlantic and the warmer Mediterranean, the peninsula becomes progressively hotter and drier from northwest to southeast. The Atlantic regions, particularly in the north and especially in Galicia, the northwest corner of Iberia, are greener and enjoy a more temperate climate with cool winters and warm summers. Because Iberia's center is so far from the coast, it is sufficiently continental that it experiences extremes ranging from snows to blistering heat. Here and toward the south and the Mediterranean Sea, the Iberian Peninsula experiences the prolonged summer dry season typical of the Mediterranean climate. If you fly here at the right time of year, you'll see the landscape transition from green to brown.

Historically, Iberia served as a crossroads for itinerants from elsewhere—Rome, Northern Europe, and Africa. While many were invaders who came only to plunder and pass on their way, many others came to settle. Millennia of cultural mixing, combined with the isolating effects of the geography, led to the

CORK OAK GROVES: Cork oak groves near the town of Vale do Pereiro in southern Portugal may at first look natural, but a closer look reveals that they are carefully managed. Regular patterns like straight lines or, as in this case, swirls conforming to hillside contours, indicate a planted forest. Cork oak grows in the western Mediterranean, especially Iberia and North Africa. Its thick outer bark can be removed every decade for up to two centuries. It has many uses, including in wine bottles—a seventeenth-century French innovation that revolutionized wine by making it possible to store and transport in bottles. Portugal produces half the world's cork total, and exports are more valuable than those of port wine. Sustainable harvesting lets this modified native ecosystem harbor extremely endangered animals like the Iberian lynx. But artificial wine stoppers could bring an end to this age-old landscape.

emergence of unique regional cultures throughout the peninsula. Several of these regions—the Basque Country, Catalonia, and Galicia among them—have held especially tightly on to their own customs, sometimes for better—fostering strong independent identities—and sometimes for worse, to the point of violence.

Portugal itself is the most dramatic example of this cultural distinctiveness. Situated on relatively low, broad lands at the western edge of Iberia, Portugal has long been focused on points outside Iberia. Its historical ties have been to its former colonies such as Brazil and to allies like England, rather than to its Iberian neighbors.

Portugal is home to the lower, navigable parts of a number of rivers that originate in Spain. The country is wetter and more mountainous in the north, and lower and drier south of the Tagus River. Flying south, you'll see the green hills of the north give way to browner lowlands.

Lisbon, the Portuguese capital, is nestled in a fine natural harbor at the mouth of the Tagus. As with many ancient cities in Iberia, and indeed throughout Europe, you'll see that the old town, with its steep and thus defensible hills, now comprises the city center. It gives way to a metropolitan sprawl that has grown to engulf several neighboring towns; about a third of the nation's people live in the greater Lisbon area, although Portugal is still one of the least urbanized countries in Europe.

You'll quickly notice the predominance of red-tiled roofs—a traditional adaptation to the heat of Southern Europe that has cooled homes here since Roman times. But the city you see today is much newer: Look for the orderly grid in the center of Lisbon's old town—unusual for ancient Iberian cities, this system was laid out in 1755 after Lisbon was demolished by an earthquake. See, too, if you can spot the green mound to the west of the old town—this is Monsanto Park, at nearly 1,000 hectares (2,500 acres) one of the largest urban parks in the world. This lush park was established in 1934 with the first forest plantings on Monsanto hill, which had been denuded by firewood gatherers.

But Lisbon was not always Portugal's social center of gravity. Algarve, the southernmost part of Portugal, was historically an important center of Portuguese imperial power in the fifteenth and sixteenth centuries. In modern times, it was a sleepy backwater until the 1970s, when the tourism industry discovered its sunny, sandy beaches and blue waters. The subsequent tourist boom has, as elsewhere in Iberia, thrown walls of hotels up behind the beaches. Nonetheless, if you're flying here you'll also see substantial protected areas atop the region's low coastal cliffs and in the coastal lagoons toward the east—critical stopover points for migratory birds on their way to and from their winter ranges in Africa.

The rest of the Iberian Peninsula is taken up by Spain. More so than most other European countries, the Spanish nation is home to sharply differentiated regions, several of which are virtually nations in their own right. The Basque

The Mediterranean—meaning "the middle of Earth" in its Latin sense—is a beautiful example of geography nurturing history. Its climate—warm and seasonally dry—and its shape—enclosed from the more ferocious oceans, and with plenty of islands and peninsulas—created the ideal conditions for the emergence of advanced human civilization.

It's possible to cross the length of the Mediterranean in many short hops, making it perfectly suited for early mariners in their primitive craft (and making it a boater's paradise today). The many islands and peninsulas meant that different peoples were isolated enough to develop distinctive cultures and yet, because of the sea routes, to trade and communicate with one another.

Because the Mediterranean's orientation is east to west, the climate is similar all along its length—and it is fortuitously located at just the right latitude to enjoy the easygoing, benevolent climate that has become synonymous with it. Characterized by a long summer dry season and a mild, wet winter, this type of climate is also found in California, Australia, South Africa, and Chile, but nowhere else is the belt so extensive as in the Mediterranean, where the sea extends its reach thousands of kilometers east from the Atlantic.

A flooded basin between the African and Eurasian plates, the Mediterranean is connected to the Atlantic through the narrow Strait of Gibraltar. This gateway to the world's oceans has been blocked off in eons past as tectonic forces jostled Earth's crust (see Plate Tectonics, page 102). During those periods, the sea dried up, creating a vast, low, salt pan with a bottom up to 3.2 kilometers (2 mi.) below sea level. The basin seems to have flooded and dried up repeatedly until about 5.4 million years ago, when the Strait of Gibraltar opened more permanently. The Mediterranean continues to be more salty than the world's oceans. At its deepest point, the Ionian Sea between Italy and Greece, the Mediterranean is 5 kilometers (3 mi.) deep, nearly half the height of the cruising altitude of your jet.

Today the Mediterranean remains an important link among countries and a critical part of the geography and ecology of Europe. Unfortunately, it has been severely damaged by human activities. Shipping, oil spills, overfishing, sewage dumping, and other insults have put the health of the sea in critical condition.

CENTER OF THE WORLD: Ibiza, a Spanish island in the Mediterranean, derived wealth for millennia from salt, the product of the rectangular evaporation ponds seen here. Built by Phoenician settlers more than 2,500 years ago, they have remained producing salt as great empires—Carthaginian, Roman, Arab—came and went. The town of Ibiza, to the north of the evaporation ponds, is the modern equivalent, hosting a raucous nightlife (including the largest nightclub on the planet) that attracts partygoers from around the world. The massive tourism industry here—the long runway at the airport can accommodate large jets flying from all over Europe and beyond—has made this unlikely island internationally known; a testament to the scale of tourism and its impact on world culture.

INDUSTRIAL PARK: South of Barcelona a major new light-industrial park is a perfect example of a type of development seen in prosperous areas throughout the world. This modern landscape features large but low and boxy buildings, plenty of road surface and parking, and virtually nothing on a human scale. It's no accident this kind of development looks exactly like the computer circuit boards that can be found somewhere in every one of these buildings: Both are attempts to optimize the distribution of processing centers on a two-dimensional grid within a connective matrix. In turn, this area is connected by the adjacent port to similar centers around the planet, a fractal relationship in the built environment that extends from the micro-scopic switches within a computer chip all the way to the global network of interconnected urban areas. These repeating patterns are a central feature of human spatial organization, and here they're on clearest display.

Country, Catalonia, Galicia, and Andalusia each manage their own affairs to differing degrees. With the emergence of an overarching European federalism in the European Union, this strong regional autonomy makes the notion of "Spain" less definitive than any other national body in Europe. As you fly across Spain, watch for changes in settlement patterns and systems of social organization from region to region. Crossing a mountain range to find a village or human landscape with different shapes and patterns than the one that came before is a good indication that you have crossed between two of Spain's autonomous communities.

Off Iberia's northern coast sits the Bay of Biscay, a shallow arm of the Atlantic underlain by part of Europe's continental shelf. The bay is rich in marine life, including many whales. From cruising altitude it's unlikely that you'll spot any, but it's always worth looking for their dark forms and white spouts if you're flying lower, as on the approach to Bilbao from the north. More likely, particularly in the summer, you'll see blooms of greenish or rust-colored plankton, swirling in gigantic eddies.

Moving west to east along this coast, you'll first encounter Galicia. Hilly and forested, with fjordlike *rías*—probing fingers of the Atlantic formed by flooded river valleys—this area is distinctively green and wet, quite different from the rest of Iberia. Northern Spain is an important fishing center, but it is also prone to coastal pollution, including big oil spills from tankers trying to skirt its rocky headlands. You're likely to see a lot of shipping in this area, although you probably won't see evidence of oil spills from the air unless one is very recent.

Next is the Asturias region, where you may spot the dramatic spires of the Picos de Europa. So named because they were often the first European landform sighted by fishermen returning from distant Atlantic fishing grounds, today these sharp limestone mountains riddled with caves are often one of the first glimpses of Iberia for travelers flying from the British Isles to Portugal. The Picos have been protected as parkland for almost a century.

Here and in the Cantabria region neighboring to the east, watch for green pasturelands in the mountains and along their flanks. With the wet, cool climate here it's no surprise the area is famed for its cheeses—many of them traditionally aged in mountain caves.

Farther east still, near the western coastal feet of the Pyrenees, where Spain's border with France comes to the Bay of Biscay, you'll see the market gardens of Navarre, an important vegetable growing region; look for neat, dark green fields. Now you are over the Basque Country, which extends south- and eastward into the mountains.

The geographical isolation of the Basque Country is plain from the air. Formidable—and beautiful—mountains separate this land from its neighbors, making it easier for the Basques to preserve their distinctive language and culture through the turbulent centuries.

The Pyrenees separate Iberia from the rest of Europe. The ridgeline forms the border between Spain and France (and houses little Andorra, a tidily settled independent principality that encompasses a single large, branched glacial valley draining south into Catalonia).

The Pyrenees are composed of rock that was once coastal plain. More than one hundred million years ago, it was pushed up into the air by tectonic collision as Iberia shoved northward into France, making the Pyrenees older than the Alps.

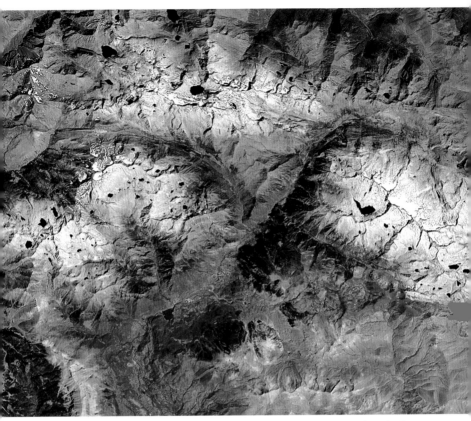

THE PYRENEES: The rugged Pyrenees show plenty of evidence of glaciation—and for now still host some of Europe's southernmost glaciers. They are a perfect example of how geography has influenced history and culture: The formidable barrier they present to cultural mixing has made them the absolute frontier between France and Spain.

For thousands of years, people on either side of this range have pursued little-connected histories. What is more, the rugged terrain has allowed highly local cultures to thrive, even into the present: The communities of the Pyrenees maintain some of Europe's most distinctive subnational identities.

Because it is the first high landform encountered by moist Atlantic winds blowing inland, the western, Basque end of the Pyrenees receives the bulk of the range's precipitation—enough that they host some of the most southerly glaciers in Europe. The largest glacier here is on Aneto (at 3,400 meters/10,000 feet the highest peak), although it is receding rapidly (see Climate Change, page 82). You can see by the numerous cirques and U-shaped valleys here that these heights were once entirely glaciated (see Glacial Terrain, page 60).

In the east, the Pyrenees become drier as they approach the Mediterranean and descend into Catalonia. This culturally distinct region is centered around the seaside city of Barcelona. Until recently the most economically dynamic part of

Spain (you'll see plenty of evidence of industry and commerce, including the many production facilities scattered throughout the city's neighborhoods), the Barcelona area remains an important center.

The coastal region from Barcelona north to the French border is the Costa Brava, one of the first and most developed of Spain's tourist areas, and one of the primary reasons that in 2002 Spain was the second most visited country on

TOURISM: A strategic point for the various maritime invaders that define Iberia's rich history, Penyal d'Ifac, a chunk of light-colored limestone jutting seaward south of Valencia, is today surrounded by intense tourist development. Like the rest of Iberia's Mediterranean coast, the Costa Blanca is a favorite place for northern Europeans—especially Britons—to escape dark, dreary winters. This rim of development places a premium on beachfront property: Often the land just behind a wall of tall hotels or dense condos is still covered in maquis or citrus. This image is also a study in water: The bright blue swimming pools contrast with the less vivid sandy-bottomed sea along the beaches. Farther out, beds of sea grass grade into deeper, darker waters. The swimming pools are signs of affluence, as is the marina crammed with pleasure boats.

Earth (after France). A favorite escape for British and German tourists, this sunny coast has been utterly transformed, both physically and culturally, from a lonely region of sleepy fishing villages. The boom started here in the 1950s, and today you'll see endless resort hotels, condos, malls, and golf courses stretching along the entire Costa Brava and south of Barcelona as well, along virtually the entire coast into Valencia and beyond to the Costa del Sol on the southern shores in Andalusia and around the horn to the Gulf of Cádiz.

The most rugged part of Iberia's Mediterranean coast is near the Sierra Nevada northeast of Málaga in Andalusia. Until recently, this area was home to Europe's southernmost glaciers; the last one melted and disappeared less than a century ago.

All along this coast, you'll see that while the beaches are crowded with tourist hotels, there are other clusters of life sitting back from the water. These are older towns and villages, often built on defensible hilltops or cliffsides. For centuries, proximity to North Africa's Barbary Coast meant that the seaboard here was infested with pirates and corsairs (state-sponsored raiders) who

SEVILLE: From the eighth century, the Moors—Muslim rulers of much of Iberia—revitalized cities like Seville while they had fallen into decay in the rest of Europe after the decline of the Roman Empire. The Moors undertook little intentional town planning, allowing their settlements to grow organically, and it was in reaction to this disorder that seven centuries later, with Seville the commercial center of Spain's global empire, authorities in the New World designed cities and towns and even villages with a single central square in which a church faces the civic administration, forming the middle of the town grid. In this image you can also see a classic feature of European cities: The main railway station is in the locus of nineteenth-century development, outside the old center (which is bounded by the ring road tracing the old city walls in Seville).

Water absorbs long wavelengths of light (which we experience as warm colors like red, orange, and yellow), so the light reflected from the water's depths is mostly of the shorter wavelengths (cool colors like blue).

Shallow areas with clear water and light bottoms—like parts of the Aegean Sea, where the seabed is composed of light-colored limestone—reflect light the most brightly. The deeper the water, therefore, the deeper the blue, with the midoceanic depths appearing very dark.

Suspended particles in water also impart color: Runoff from the surrounding land gives many rivers a matching color. (Glacial streams, for example, are often milky with fine silt.) Watch for places where bodies of water containing different-colored particles come together, and you'll be able to see how they mix.

Greens are usually due to algae, while plankton, bacteria, and red algae cause the bright reds you sometimes see in salt-evaporation ponds and warm ocean waters.

Ice and snow appear white, as when pack ice accumulates on large bodies of water like the northern reaches of the Baltic Sea or the Arctic Ocean. Look for jagged white shards separated by raised seams.

combed the region for plunder and captives. Avoiding vulnerable coastal locations became a matter of survival for communities here; some of these settlements are walled for the same reason. You may also be able to see that the shore is lined with slender watchtowers, another antipiracy measure.

Andalusia, Spain's southernmost region, is perhaps Iberia's most historically dynamic. A longtime Roman stronghold, the region also spent seven centuries (ending in the fifteenth century) as a bastion of Islamic Moorish culture centered in Seville, situated on the Guadalquivir River. Later, during Spain's colonial period, Andalusia was the gateway to the Americas—indeed, Columbus's famous expedition to the New World left from this region in 1492. If you're flying from Iberia to the Americas today, consider that the journey that may take you as little as five hours took him five weeks.

The lands sloping north and south of the Guadalquivir River are extensively irrigated, as you can see by the lushly green but sharply demarcated farmland that contrasts with the dry countryside. This is not unusual in Spain, where the dry climate precludes depending on rainfall for agriculture: Because of their proximity to fresh water, the shoulders of Iberia's rivers are the peninsula's richest farmland. Throughout Iberia you'll see reservoirs where river valleys have been dammed to provide irrigation water (see Water Systems, page 52).

Though far inland, Seville is the most important port in the region. The Spanish treasure fleet from the Americas landed here from the sixteenth to eighteenth centuries, laden with gold, silver, chocolate, tobacco, and much else. During this time, Andalusia was one of the richest regions in Europe—indeed, the world. Signs of this era of prosperity you can see from the air include the sumptuous cathedrals at the center of any sizable town; Seville's is the largest in the world.

At the mouth of the Guadalquivir, the land lies low and marshy, and much of it is used to cultivate rice. Look for regular plots of uniform green, often reflecting light from their flooded surfaces. Like most of Spain's waters, the Guadalquivir is quite polluted by industrial and municipal effluent and agricultural runoff. While conditions are improving here (it was only in preparation for the 1992 Olympics that Barcelona, a city of 1.5 million, finally began to treat its sewage), Spain has long been home to some of the most polluted spots in Western Europe.

The center of the Iberian Peninsula also houses an assortment of distinct regions, usually formed around the irrigable lands along the rivers. Historically, however, the centers of power sat near the coasts. To counterbalance the competing coastal regions, Madrid, perched on a high plateau right in the middle of the peninsula (at 646 meters, or 2,120 ft., it is the highest European capital), was designated in the ninth century by the Moors as a political center. For centuries, through the Moorish and Christian empires, it survived as a courtly city, depending on tribute from surrounding regions. Only in the

IRRIGATION: In areas with irregular or seasonal rainfall, such as along the banks of the Río Tajo west of Toledo, irrigation is the only way to keep thirsty crops green. These circles are the result of center-pivot irrigation, in which a long rotating arm on wheels sprays water from a central well. In areas with rougher terrain or different amounts of available water, other forms of irrigation are used. In all cases, the telltale sign of irrigation is lush green cropland amid a dry landscape. Note the reservoir and canal in this image—in the Mediterranean climate, water management is critical to virtually all human activity. Indeed, people have been irrigating for at least seven thousand years, making this technology one of the oldest and most important elements of human civilization.

twentieth century, under the direction of the Fascist dictator Franco, did Madrid develop any industry. Now it is Iberia's leading economic center, which you'll see clearly if you fly over this region and one of the major sites of suburban sprawl in Spain, a problem that is more common here than in the rest of Europe. Also look for the many grand projects that define the twentieth-century parts of the city, like the sweeping avenues of the Cementerio sur de Carabanchel, at the south end of the city.

As greenhouse gases like carbon dioxide accumulate in the atmosphere from human activities, Earth's climate is changing. Scientists predict that this will mean warmer temperatures around the globe in the coming century, but the specific changes felt in any one place will depend on complicated factors including geography, proximity to the ocean, and shifts in ocean currents and weather patterns.

Compared to other parts of the world, Europe is particularly threatened by climate change. Its southern reaches sit at the edge of a dry region that leads into the parched Sahara Desert in Africa. Heating of the atmosphere could bring those conditions northward, threatening to render agriculture more difficult in places like southern Spain. Summers there are already hotter and drier than ever before—in the last century, average temperatures throughout the EU have risen nearly 1°C (2°F), but the increase has been up to twice that in parts of Spain, where rainfall has dropped by 25 percent in the past three decades.

One effect of this increased dryness has been a rise in the number of wildfires in the Iberian Peninsula. If you're flying over the region during the summer, you may be able to see a wildfire in progress (check regional news reports before you fly so you'll know where to look). Watch for plumes of whitish smoke rising from forestland. The smoke travels great distances, so when you spot smoke—usually either drifting like low, dirty stratus clouds (horizontal clouds that spread across the sky like a blanket) or billowing upward—try to follow it back to its source: That's a wildfire.

Conversely, northwestern Europe is warmed by Atlantic currents that bring tropical waters far to the north, thus keeping the British Isles and the coast of Norway ice-free during the winter. Disruption of this current by melting polar ice caps or other changes could bring these regions' climate more into line with other places at similar latitudes—places like Siberia and Alaska.

Higher temperatures are already melting glaciers around the world. The Aneto Glacier, in the Pyrenees, will be gone in a few decades. Many Scandinavian and Alpine

(continued)

POLLUTION: Heaps of coal, blackened factories, and abandoned lots characterize the depressed industrial area of Silesia in southern Poland. Long prosperous, even before the discovery of coal in the region and the subsequent boom in heavy industry in the nineteenth century, Silesia has fallen into decay since the collapse of the Iron Curtain exposed its inefficient Communist-era facilities to global competition. Communist factories were among the most polluting in the world, rendering this region black with soot and reducing life expectancy. In 1991 this area was officially declared an ecological disaster zone. Though the demise of industry has thrown thousands out of work, it has improved health in the region by clearing the air. Eventually, Silesia's natural advantages should help it recover: With Polish membership in the EU, Western corporations are establishing cleaner industrial facilities in this region.

glaciers are also receding. These changes are altering local ecosystems and, as the massive polar ice caps themselves begin to melt, may raise sea levels around the world—a possibility that is being met with real alarm in low-lying countries like the Netherlands, nearly half of which is currently 1 meter (3 ft.) above sea level or lower.

While the world has been warming naturally since the end of the Pleistocene Ice Age some 10,000 years ago, the pace of warming has increased dramatically since the start of the Industrial Revolution. This is because the burning of fossil fuels like coal and oil has increased the concentration of carbon dioxide in the atmosphere by some 40 percent in the past 150 years—a change to the makeup of our planet whose effects are already clearly visible from above, and that may ultimately threaten our very survival.

Humanity has found itself in a conundrum, for our civilization is founded on the burning of fossil fuels. One round-trip flight across the Atlantic, for example, adds three tons of carbon to the atmosphere for each passenger, yet the benefits are undeniable: five hours of high-altitude relaxation surely beats the five months of toil on a leaking sailboat it took early explorers to make the same crossing.

As one of the richest regions on Earth, Europe is responsible for more than its fair share of carbon emissions. But because of its geography it is also among the most susceptible to deleterious climate change effects like rising sea levels, drying, and the disruption of ocean currents—an irony that has spurred these powerful nations to action long before other major carbon emitters.

ITALY

WATCH FOR

GEOLOGICAL FEATURES				
		Volcanoes	Mountains	Valleys

HYDROLOGICAL FEATURES			
		Marshes	Rugged Coasts

ECOLOGICAL FEATURES			
		Forests	Marshes

HUMAN FEATURES			
Canals	Towns in Unlikely Places	Farmland	Ancient Settlement Patterns

BONUS SIGHTS
Florence, Genoa, San Marino, Elba, industrial centers

A long, uniformly narrow peninsula jutting southward into the Mediterranean, Italy is the dramatic result of the ongoing slow-motion collision between the African tectonic plate and the Eurasian plate that it continues to rise over (see Plate Tectonics, page 102). This roiling geological saga is reflected in Italy's lively volcanoes and hot springs today. Mount Etna in Sicily, for example, is one of the most active volcanoes in the world and Vulcano, a volcanic island off Sicily, named after the Roman metalworking god of the underworld, is eponymous for these fiery mountains.

Italy's volcanoes cluster mostly along the western side of the peninsula, which stretches from southern Tuscany to Naples and also around Sicily. The volcanic systems here are extremely complex, with volcanoes in close proximity often arising from different underlying phenomena—a situation rarely found elsewhere.

PO VALLEY: Cremona, a little more than 100 kilometers (60 mi.) from Milan, was established as a Roman military outpost in 218 BCE on the site of a Gaul settlement. It still features an orderly downtown grid around the two axial roads that led to the four city gates. Cremona became an important regional center, as evidenced by the radial pattern of roads and fields around it, connecting the rich farmland of the Plain of Lombardy with the Po River. Like medieval cities throughout Europe, Cremona developed its own urban economy of craft and manufacture, eventually becoming a major center with a larger population than its current 70,000. Rather than the area's rich farmland, the resources that attracted modern development like the oil terminal to the west of the town are the established transportation links and the people of Cremona themselves, who provide a workforce.

To pick out volcanoes from the air, watch for conical, pointed mountains that rise sharply above the surrounding countryside. Craters at the mountains' summits and lava flows—rock that once oozed out of the mountain and is now solidified in shapes that bespeak its liquid origins—give away volcanoes. If they are particularly active you may even see steam or smoke coming from their tops. Watch, too, for the black volcanic soils that help make Italy such an agriculturally productive country.

The Apennines, the long ridge of mountains that forms Italy's backbone, stretches more than a thousand kilometers (600 mi.), from Liguria to Calabria and into Sicily, and includes a few high rocky peaks like Gran Sasso in Abruzzi, northeast of Rome. At nearly 3,000 meters (10,000 ft.), Gran Sasso hosts, for now, Europe's southernmost glacier (see Climate Change, page 82). But for the most part the Apennines are low and rugged and are covered in vegetation.

If you fly into Italy from the north, you'll notice immediately that the Alps give way suddenly to the expansive flatness of the Po River Valley. Protected from cold northern winds by the Alps, this is Italy's agricultural and industrial heartland. Although it comprises only a quarter of the country, it houses half of the nation's workforce and is responsible for 40 percent of the country's economic output.

Because the historically great trading city of Venice sits at the mouth of the Po, many different elements of far-off cultures became part of life here centuries ago. From the air, you'll see one example. This area is heavily cultivated—the flat, irrigated land is perfect for all sorts of crops—and one of the major crops is rice, a staple introduced to Europe by Arab traders who had originally acquired it in India. Look for emerald green, often flooded fields in summer.

The extensive industrial development that has taken place in the Po Valley over the past two centuries is also clearly visible from on high. Turin, with its ring of picturesque and rugged mountains, has long been Italy's automotive and aerospace center. Nearby Milan lies on the Plain of Lombardy, in the center of Italy's most economically developed region. Milan is the country's financial center and the fourth-largest metropolitan area in Western Europe. In both cases, you'll see that these cities have grown unimpeded by natural barriers and extend nearly uniformly in all directions.

The hydrological cycles in the Po Valley are dramatic. If you're flying past the valley's northern Alpine side, you'll see five huge lakes (including famous Lake Como), formed behind moraines that serve as natural dams at the mouths of glacial valleys (see Glacial Terrain, page 60). You can also spot alluvial fans—cone-shaped areas of debris that have been deposited where mountain rivers empty onto the flat plain at the basin's floor. Sediment deposited here from the uplands all around the basin make it rich and easily worked farmland. Where the Po enters the waters of the Adriatic Sea, its delta forms a dynamic estuary, though one troubled by pollution and interrupted natural cycles.

Throughout the valley, humans have altered the Po to suit their needs. In addition to the reservoirs and hydroelectric dams (see Water Systems, page 52) that provide most of the region's power, you'll see levees—straight manmade banks that, at least when they are working properly, limit the river's natural springtime tendency to flood. And on the coast just north of the delta you'll see Venice, one of the most celebrated examples of humankind's audacious experiments with changing the world to suit our needs.

Venice sits precariously on a set of marshy islands in a lagoon at the top of the Adriatic. Established here in the sixth century in an effort to avoid land-based enemies, Venice became an important marine trading power in the Middle Ages. Its wealth was legendary, and its influence spread throughout the Mediterranean. Napoleon brought the thousand-year reign of this commercial empire to an end when he finally conquered the republic two hundred years ago.

More recently, of course, Venice has become one of the world's most renowned tourist destinations, although this, too, has brought its challenges. Fifteen million visitors swarm the city each year, dwarfing its permanent population of sixty thousand (and falling) and jamming its narrow alleyways and piazzas with noisy crowds—one of the world's premier examples of mass tourism destroying the very thing that attracts visitors to begin with.

Worse, river diversion projects that reduce sediment entering the lagoon, as well as the removal of underground water for irrigation and industry on the nearby mainland, have caused Venice's low islands to subside even as sea levels rise, threatening the city with permanent inundation.

Still, Venice's creaking infrastructure has a charming look. It is Europe's largest car-free urban zone, with canals and footbridges linking its one hundred islands, each jammed with unique architecture. In an effort to save the city, the Italian government has begun the Moses Project, an innovative system of movable underwater dams designed to block Adriatic storm surges—a modern continuation of historical projects to maintain the lagoon in the city's favor. Look for construction barges near the mouths of the lagoon.

To the south of the Po Valley, across the Apennines, you'll see the green (or golden, in summer) rolling hills of Tuscany. The home of the Italian Renaissance and an important historical center in the development of Western culture, Tuscany is also a major tourist draw. From the air its landscape of small, red-roofed towns, hills capped with villas ensconced in plantings of Lombardy poplars, vineyards, and olive groves demonstrate why this region is the epitome of romantic Italy.

Italy's legion olive groves have helped define the cuisine here for nearly three thousand years. Watch for rows (sometimes ragged) of, well, olive green shrubby trees, often on steep ground. In particular, watch for olive groves near the sea and on the lighter-colored soils of central Italy (arising from weathering of the limestone mountains in the area).

Agricultural patterns that date back millennia define the rural landscape throughout Italy. Ninety-five percent of the farms here are family-owned. Even in the face of growing international competition, Italian and European policies protect this traditional arrangement. Still, the remaining 5 percent of farms are much bigger, accounting for a third of the country's farmland.

VENICE: Venice is legendary as the city of canals, and here, at the edge of the city, you can see this in practice: Boats serve in the role played by cars in virtually every other city. The wide expanse of water is the Venice Lagoon, which is a sheltered estuary connected to the Adriatic Sea. The boat traffic here is heavy as well—the long white wakes indicate that these vessels are moving quickly; you can judge the relative speeds of boats by the length and sharpness of their wakes: Faster and heavier boats leave longer wakes. Note the red-tiled roofs: Throughout the Mediterranean, these tiles mirror the color of the local clay and provide a climate-appropriate roofing material for the hot, sunny region while making the landscape even more appealing.

From above you'll plainly see that Italy has plenty of wildlands, too: From the Po Basin to Calabria, the mountains are often heavily forested with the sort of tough, evergreen oak forest adapted to this climate with its hot, dry summers. At middle elevations you'll see lighter-leaved beech forests blanketing the slopes; in the winter these trees lose their leaves while the oaks lower down and conifers higher up do not.

THE APENNINES: The town of Andronoco (population 2,800), in the Apennines north of Rome, is surrounded by native beech forest, rocky mountains (snow covered in winter), and hot springs. Because of its strategic location at the confluence of two valleys, Andronoco has been settled for millennia. In Roman times the sulphurous springs made this a destination for urban dwellers seeking to get away from the rigors of the city, a distinction this area enjoys once again today. The different layers of history since the Roman period can still be seen on the landscape. In contrast to the classic Roman layout of the old town center, the DVX of trees planted below the peak of Monte Giano in 1939 is a reminder of how ephemeral empires can be. DVX was Latin for Mussolini's de facto title—il Duce.

Though some of this woodland is old, virtually primeval forest, much of it grew in the early part of the twentieth century, when thousands of people left the land to seek opportunity in Italy's cities—a process that continues as the population concentrates along the west coast. The absence of farming allowed forests to grow, creating the modern wilderness in these mountains. Centuries of livestock grazing accounts for the remaining pastureland at higher elevations.

At the pivot point of the long Italian Peninsula sits Rome, Italy's largest city. The greatest city in Europe for nearly a thousand years before the Middle Ages (indeed the greatest in the world for much of that time), Rome is Italy's capital, although its contemporary power is balanced by other strong regional centers. Modern Rome exhibits layer upon layer of history in almost every aspect, and from the air you can see the characteristic patterns of different epochs of city planning (or lack of planning) side by side. For example, if you can spot the Vatican, the city-within-a-city that is the seat of the Roman

Catholic Church (and which is, legally, the smallest country in the world), you'll see that its sweeping baroque form contrasts with the apparent chaos of the ancient center directly across the river, as well as with the blocky, linear Fascist-era avenue that connects the two quarters.

Today the old center, parts of which date back two thousand years or more, is surrounded by different additions that date from the last few hundred years, and in particular the last century. Perhaps most intriguing is the modernist 1930s Fascist suburb of EUR (an acronym for Esposizione Universale Romana, an event that never took place). South of Rome's center, EUR is positioned roughly between Rome's two airports, so watch for its distinctive broad streets lined with leafy trees and the studied curves of its artificial lake if you fly in or out of Rome.

Though plenty of people commute into the city center—the number of people in Rome increases by about a million during the day—most of them come from surrounding communities that are established cities and towns in their own right. Rome so far has been spared the halo of sprawling new development that has afflicted cities like London and Madrid.

Along the coast here and southward on both sides of the peninsula, to Naples in the west and all the way to Apulia in the east, you'll see flat coastal lands heavily settled and cultivated. For centuries these areas were inhospitable marshlands; ancient Rome was plagued by malaria before the Pontine Marshes south of the city were drained. In the past century, almost all the remaining marshes have been drained, creating an entirely new type of Italian landscape. Look for drainage canals running in straight lines across these lands. (In the Apennines you can also see a few flat cultivated areas where lakes have been drained.)

Otherwise, the Italian coastline is for the most part extremely rugged, as in Liguria around Genoa or the Amalfi coast south of Naples. Here the mountains plunge straight into the sea, forcing human settlement to cling to the most improbable-looking seaside toeholds. Watch for towns like Positano that seem to spill directly into the sea like blocky, pastel landslides of antique human endeavor. Such towns and cities historically faced the sea for their livelihoods of fishing and trading.

From Campania southward, you'll be flying over the Mezzogiorno—the least-developed part of Italy. Hotter and drier than areas to the north, you'll see that this region is largely treeless: It was deforested by early inhabitants like similar heavily grazed, arid areas in the Balkans, with resulting erosion. In antiquity, this area was settled by Phoenicians and Greeks, and cities here like Naples and Palermo on the island of Sicily date to that period. The region has also had much interchange with African and Arab cultures.

ROME: The most historic spot in a continent saturated in history, Rome was a locus of power for a thousand years. For four hundred it presided over all of Western Europe and the Mediterranean. A city of over a million people at its ancient peak, Rome was the largest city in the world at the time. (Four million people live in modern Rome's metropolitan area.) Ancient Rome confronted urban problems that still plague us: The city's first sewer system was built 2,600 years ago. Famous relics, including the Coliseum, the Circus Maximus, and the Pantheon, all of which can be seen in this image, still define the city's character. Even after the fall of the empire, the Vatican—the keyhole-shaped complex—remained the seat of the pope, commanding the allegiance of most of Europe for another millennium. Today, the Vatican is technically an independent country and remains the center of the Roman Catholic Church.

MONTE NUOVO: During a single week in 1538, Monte Nuovo erupted on the coast near Naples, at the center of one of the most volcanically active places in the world. The youngest mountain in Europe, Monte Nuovo is a type of volcano called a cinder cone. It consists of light, frothy magma blown in a fiery fountain out of a volcanic vent. Though it is small by Italian standards, it illustrates perfectly how perilous volcanism can be for human settlement: The eruption engulfed one village and forced the abandonment of another. (Pompeii, the famous Roman city destroyed by an eruption in 79 CE, is nearby.) But Monte Nuovo also shows how compelling volcanoes can be, even for people who know the risks: Volcanic soil is excellent for agriculture, and the forces that create volcanoes can also produce beneficial features like hot springs. In this region, people crowd around them.

In the past two centuries, the Mezzogiorno has been the source of much emigration to northern Italy (fifteen million people after World War II alone), particularly the Po Valley. Many also went abroad: Most people of Italian descent in the New World can trace their roots to the Mezzogiorno. The region continues to be troubled, as development is ill-planned and increasing climate change-related drought threatens the agricultural region's already faltering economy.

Across Europe remain traces both obvious and subtle of ancient civilizations. The landscape you see from your plane is the result of thousands of years of human intervention, and much of what came before is still visible. In many regions, settlement still follows patterns laid out in the distant past—after all, good harbors, fertile plains, and transportation routes like mountain passes and navigable rivers appeal to many different kinds of societies in many different ages.

What's more, once a settlement has been established, it takes a compelling reason to abandon a good site with all that infrastructure. Thus present-day European settlement patterns reflect decisions dating back millennia. For example, it was during the time of the Roman Empire, which at its height nearly two thousand years ago stretched from near the Caspian Sea to the Atlantic and from North Africa to the British Isles, that key decisions about the human settlement of much of Europe were made.

Thousands of townsites—including some that became major modern cities, such as London—were established by the Romans, as were roadways, bridges, and other infrastructure like aqueducts. Today their work can still be seen in not only the choice of locations, but also the layouts of town centers—look for the typical Roman grid pattern with a central square, a design based on Roman military camps as well as earlier antecedents, like Greek cities (see Cremona on page 86). (Rome itself does not fully display this plan, as it was founded before this imperial system was developed.) This basic layout has been adapted by many subsequent planners in Europe and elsewhere, as have other Roman innovations, like the long, straight roadways favored by imperial engineers.

During later periods, different planning motivations held sway. In the unstable Middle Ages, when towns were largely on their own—that is, without the protection of powerful states—and were frequently threatened by marauders, settlements were built with defense in mind. Walled cities sprang up on higher ground, often with a cathedral in the center. You can easily see many of these from the air today—look for tall, pointed spires in densely packed small towns overlooking agricultural areas.

(continued)

THE WANDLEBURY RING: The remains of an Iron Age hill fort built in the fifth century BCE are visible in the East Anglian countryside. Throughout this landscape are conspicuous mounds and knolls—the remains of prehistoric, Roman, and more recent constructions (old canals and rail lines and World War II airfields are particularly visible in England). Here, marks in the fields reveal old roads, boundaries, and drainages.

The telltale fairways, roughs, and sand traps of the Gog Magog Golf Club do not seem out of place, for they are approximations of the similar moist postglacial landscape found in golf's native Scotland. But as golf has spread around the world (initially aided by the British Empire: the first golf club outside Great Britain was in Bangalore), such simulated glacial terrain is now incongruously found in deserts, tropical regions, and anywhere else this unlikely sport has flourished.

But Europe is also littered with abundant evidence of far, far older societies. Discerning—and lucky—window gazers can even spot elements from Neolithic (late Stone Age) cultures, such as ceremonial sites like the circular henges of Great Britain that date back five thousand years or more.

The attributes that make modern human impacts on the landscape stand out from the air can signal older human features as well. Trace remains of straight lines, circles, and regular patterns are still good signs that *something* human-made is or was down there, although further evidence that clarifies just what may be obscured. The human touch can be manifested subtly in the vegetation or colors of the ground, sometimes visible only at certain times of the year or day. The low setting sun, for example, can highlight patterns within a crop field. Bands of plants of a slightly different height or color from neighbors in the same field may be a sign of something beneath. Perhaps they're growing in the enriched soil of a World War I trenchline in Belgium, or the more challenging conditions above the foundations of a forgotten Roman palace in southern France.

Indeed, the perspective offered when it first became possible to contemplate the land from above engendered a renaissance in archaeology. Britain, with more than eighty years of systematic civilian aerial photography, is the most surveyed in this way. In the 1980s, for instance, a mapping effort in the Yorkshire Wolds revealed an unsuspected richness of prehistoric, Roman, and medieval traces, including field boundaries, farmsteads, roadways, and more. In response, an aerial archaeological survey was completed for all of England.

Restrictions on civilian flights and aerial photography elsewhere, including the former Communist countries and also archaeological treasure troves like Spain and Greece, have hampered this kind of work in the recent past, but the situation is changing: Italy opened its skies to aerial archaeologists in 2000, for example. Nonetheless, it is still possible for the keen-eyed layperson to spot something the experts haven't.

THE BALKAN PENINSULA

GEOLOGICAL FEATURES

		Sharp Ridges	Valleys	Thousands of Rugged Islands
		⋀	∨	☁☁

HYDROLOGICAL FEATURES

				Rugged Coastline
				ح

ECOLOGICAL FEATURES

		Scrublands	Alpine Meadows	Forests
		♥♥♥♥♥♥	⏸	🌲

HUMAN FEATURES

			Remote Towns	Bomb Damage
			⌐	🂠

BONUS SIGHTS

The Rila Mountains, Mount Olympus, NATO military bases, isolated villages

Europe's seemingly endless history of conquest, migration, and shifting borders is nowhere more dramatic—and troubling—than in the Balkan Peninsula. A big jumble of steep mountains, the region is known for its great diversity of cultural enclaves. Flying over this region, it's easy to see how this "Balkanization" happened.

Most Balkan towns and cities lie in valleys and basins between mountain ridges. These fertile and habitable lands have attracted settlers for at least 200,000 years. But because travel through this rugged terrain is so difficult—just imagine trying to cross the steep and craggy mountains on foot—the successive waves of migration and conquest over the millennia have left dozens of pockets of vastly different cultures, each with their own language, ethnicity, and religion. Isolated from one another by the landscape, these groups rarely intermixed, contributing to a history of mutual suspicion, even in areas where they lived side by side. This tension came to the fore when Yugoslavia

DUBROVNIK: Dubrovnik, a medieval city on the Dalmatian coast in present-day Croatia, was the seat of a powerful maritime republic for four hundred years, a regional rival of Venice until Napoleon seized them both in 1806. It displays the classic defensive layout of a compact center enclosed in tall walls. Today improved with a breakwater—the long bar of fill—this pretty harbor is a favorite destination of pleasure boaters, as you can see by the many white yachts and sailboats. Inland, notice how steeply the Dalmatian mountains rise up from this coast, and how barren and inhospitable they are after millennia of grazing. The dark water reveals that this steepness extends out to sea—the deepest part of the Mediterranean is not far away. The image also shows an interference pattern in the waves that have been refracted around an island just off the coast.

disintegrated in the 1990s, and the long-held hostilities in the region erupted into violence. The first war in Europe since World War II, this conflict ruined millions of lives and the economy of this beautiful and fascinating country.

While the extreme poverty in places like Albania—nearly half the people there subsist on less than two euros per day—is partly the result of the painful transition away from Communism, regionwide economic sluggishness dates back to the nineteenth century, the time of the Ottoman Empire. This Turkish empire included the Balkans for half a millennium, from the fourteenth to the nineteenth century, during which little development took place in this inaccessible backwater, far from the center of power in Turkey. For centuries, Belgrade, Skopje, and Sofia were the only metropolitan cities in the region. You can spot signs of the Ottoman Empire here and there in town layouts: Look for central squares where bazaars were held, as well as domed mosques, especially in the towns of Turkish-dominated southern Bulgaria.

When the Industrial Revolution swept northern Europe, the Balkans remained stuck in the past. It was only after World War II, when the region (excluding Greece) fell under the sway of vigorously proindustrial Communists that any significant industrial development took place, thanks to subsidies from the Soviet Union.

That explains the noticeably bucolic landscape you can see from above. Shepherds still guide their flocks through the high mountains in summer, and tiny agricultural villages dot the hillsides. Communist planners often sited facilities with little regard to economic realities, so you'll see here and there factories seated incongruously in the middle of farm towns, a local manifestation of a pattern seen more commonly in Eastern Europe and Russia. Now usually idle, these boxy buildings and their smokestacks are telltale signs of the Communist period (see Central Planning, page 146).

ATHENS: Though Athens is one of the oldest cities in the world, and most likely the oldest continuously inhabited European city, modern Athens is decidedly new: Its basic plan was laid out after Greek independence in 1832 and most of the present sprawl arose only in the past fifty years. Throughout the six thousand years of Athens' history, Piraeus, shown here, was the city's port. Though Athens proper is located inland, the two cities are now completely contiguous. Indeed, the entire plain of Athens is solidly urbanized. In the fifth century BCE, Piraeus became the first city to be laid out on a grid pattern—an innovation that has echoed through history and around the world. The original port was at the smallest harbor seen here. The modern port, Greece's largest, is at the top left of this image.

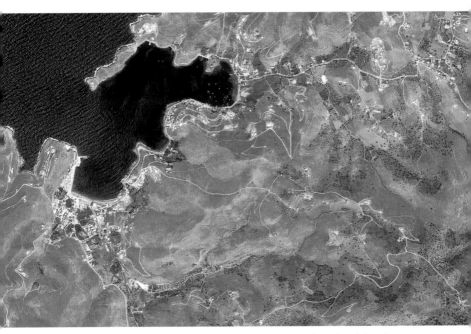

GREEK ISLAND: Though the island of Kéa is not far from the most heavily populated part of Greece, it embodies a rugged remoteness that evokes the mythical significance of the Greek Islands. From the air, you can see how well this region lent itself to a nascent seafaring people: It has plenty of placid coves, predictable winds, and short distances between islands equipped with fertile inland valleys. These same features make the Greek Islands a pleasure boater's paradise today: Watch for telltale white yachts and sailboats, a few of which can be seen here in the calm harbor of Vourkari.

Because of the lack of well-planned industrial development, large swaths of the Balkans remain as they did hundreds of years ago. The Dalmatian coast, on the eastern side of the Adriatic Sea (and home of the eponymous dogs), is dotted with tiny fishing villages and towns. Ancient Roman and Greek ports nestle among coves that, before the tragic 1990s, made this one of the most visited parts of Communist Europe. Magnificently unspoiled, this coast will inevitably return to prominence as a favorite tourist destination.

The steep uplands inland from the Dalmatian coast are made of limestone (you can tell by their light color) and have been weathered by eons of rain that formed caves and sinkholes. Watch for abrupt depressions in the landscape where cave ceilings have collapsed.

You'll also see that the mountains throughout the southern parts of the Balkan Peninsula—the Dalmatian coast south through Greece—tend to be drier. They're only lightly vegetated with scrubby maquis, coarse woodlands of evergreen shrubs. This wasn't always the case; prior to humans' arrival, the land was forested. Early deforestation followed by millennia of grazing by goats and sheep led to the change in the landscape.

Dry, steep, and hard to farm, the Mediterranean region of the peninsula is nonetheless widely agricultural. Most production takes place in irrigated valleys—watch for flat green patches as you fly above, particularly in the summer when the mountains tend toward a dry brown.

Inland, north and toward the Black Sea—roughly Sarajevo (the capital of Bosnia) east through Serbia and Bulgaria—you'll notice more densely forested land and lush farms. In this region, the Balkans descend into the fertile Alföld (the Hungarian Plain) and the Danube valley.

Bulgaria, which was spared the catastrophe of war in the 1990s but which nonetheless suffers from economic difficulties in the wake of the collapse of Communism, is the most fertile part of the Balkans. Flying above, you'll see huge farms assembled through Communist collectivization, as well as smaller holdings surrounding picturesque villages in the rolling landscapes of the country's broad valleys. This region, as well as European Turkey and part of northern Greece, is ancient Thrace, where the secrets of Dionysus were kept hidden in the Rhodope Mountains.

While Greece sits in the southernmost corner of the Balkans, it's the most "Westernized," in the sense that it never fell under Communist rule. When economic development came here after World War II, it came quickly. Athens is today a sprawling metropolis gobbling up neighboring cities in a megalopolis of more than three million people. (In 1830, when Greece gained its independence from the Ottoman Empire, Athens' inhabitants numbered just five thousand.) If you fly into its airport, you'll be able to see the results of this tremendous growth: Look for compact old town centers engulfed in a matrix of modern development hemmed in only by the sea and mountains. Piraeus, ancient Athens' port city, for example, is now a contiguous part of the metropolis.

A major tourist destination, Greece welcomes almost fifteen million visitors each year. It was the cradle of Western civilization, with the city-state of Athens the birthplace of many of the currents of Western thought. As you fly here, or over the thousands of tiny islands dotting the blue Aegean Sea, think about the ancient legends that sprang from this place. This is the sea upon which the Iliad played out, and where Odysseus, perhaps the greatest traveler of all, wandered for years, seeking his way back home.

Toward the east lies Turkey, the last Muslim nation with a toehold in Europe. A remnant of the Ottoman presence here, Turkey remains the gateway to the East and regrettably out of the scope of this book.

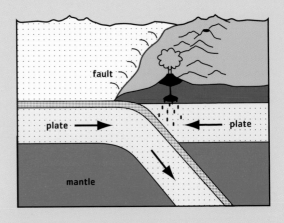

Like a profiterole, our planet has a gooey center—a metal core surrounded by a mantle of liquid rock called magma (this is the stuff that comes spewing out of volcanoes). Floating on top of this mantle are tectonic plates—solid rock that forms Earth's crust. In areas where the crust is very thick, a continental plate juts skyward and forms dry land. Thinner oceanic crust is found deep beneath the seas.

In most parts of Europe, Earth's crust is more than 30 kilometers (20 mi.) thick, but under the Atlantic Ocean it averages just 6 kilometers (4 mi.)—less than the height of your plane above Earth's surface at cruising altitude.

Currents in the mantle jostle the plates above them, and their collisions create the most spectacular geological features. Mountain ranges form where plates collide or slide over one another, and the most dramatic geological events—including earthquakes and volcanic eruptions—are evidence of this relentless process.

Because the plates move constantly, the positions of the continents and oceans on Earth change dramatically over the course of millions of years. Today's world map is just a snapshot of an ongoing rearrangement that can bring regions together or tear them apart and distribute them to opposite sides of the planet. (The ancient uplands of northern Britain, for example, were once contiguous with similar formations in North America.)

The most active part of the continent is in the south, where the African plate has been pushing up and over the Eurasian plate for more than twenty million years. This action piles debris onto the Eurasian plate, giving rise to the sharp peaks of the Alps, the Apennines, the Carpathians, and the Balkan Mountains. This process continues today, with the mountains rising at up to a centimeter each year.

THE CENTER

North
Sea

Baltic Sea

GERMANY

Hamburg

Berlin

RUHR RIVER

RHINE RIVER

Frankfurt

POLAND

Warsaw

CENTRAL EUROPE

Prague

**CZECH
REPUBLIC**

Munich

SWITZERLAND

Geneva

DANUBE RIVER

Vienna

SLOVAKIA

Budapest

HUNGARY

AUSTRIA

THE ALPS

MOLDOVA

CARPATHIANS

Bucharest

ROMANIA

THE CENTER

GERMANY

			GEOLOGICAL FEATURES	
		Moraines	Plains	Mountains

			HYDROLOGICAL FEATURES	
Lakes	Big Rivers	Circular Crater Lakes in Old Volcanoes		Marshes

			ECOLOGICAL FEATURES	
			Marshes	Evergreen Forests

			HUMAN FEATURES	
Roads	Canals	Cities	Towns	Mines

BONUS SIGHTS
Munich, Berlin, Hamburg, Frankfurt, the Black Forest, the Mittelland Canal, Autobahns

No matter which direction you fly over Germany—and you could be coming from any point on the compass, as Germany is quite literally Europe's heartland—you'll see a charmingly patterned settled land, largely agricultural but punctuated throughout with towns and large cities. Depending on which region you're above—the flat coastal plain, the rolling central uplands, or the more rugged Alpine region—the details will differ. But this typically German arrangement, while found elsewhere in Europe, is nowhere so widespread over a country of this size. Germany boasts the largest economy in Europe and the third largest in the world. In the west and the south (and also increasingly in the east), you'll see hallmarks of great wealth along with enduring evidence of this country's troubled history.

Germany rises gradually from the North and Baltic Seas, then more sharply south toward the Alps. Northern Germany is part of the North European Plain, a low-lying area of glacial till stretching from the Low Countries all the way to the Ural Mountains in the middle of Eurasia. Left behind by receding glaciers more than ten thousand years ago, this region is riddled with classic lowland glacial features: Look for long moraines running east-west, ponds, eskers, and wide glacial spillways that now form the broad valleys of much smaller rivers (see Glacial Terrain, page 60). In Brandenburg, the region that

MORAINES: In Brandenburg, north of Berlin, the North European Plain is marked by long rows of huge moraines left behind by the retreating ice sheet ten thousand years ago. Here, the moraine runs from the top left to the bottom right of the image. It is forested while much of the plains around it are farmed. Running in parallel lines, these wide ridges mark the edges of a great ice sheet that was once centered in the Baltic Sea, far to the north. Other glacial features abound here too, especially numerous kettle ponds left behind by chunks of ice melting in the sandy glacial till.

surrounds Berlin, as well as farther north near the coast in Mecklenburg, you'll see some of the finest examples of this landscape.

The plain's North Sea coast is low and swampy—you'll see flat expanses of reclaimed farmland protected from the sea in the manner perfected in the Low Countries (see pages 49–56). The Baltic coast features limestone cliffs worn by glaciation—white cliffs that you may be able to spot if you fly over the coast here.

This region hosts Germany's largest ports—Hamburg, which is the second-largest container port in Europe, and Bremen. Their locations are not accidents. Each of these cities, located near the mouths of two of Germany's great rivers—the Elbe and the Weser, respectively—have historically served the broad basins of these two rivers. It's similarly no accident that Germany's largest port isn't in Germany: Rotterdam, in the Netherlands, handles much of Germany's traffic due to its position at the mouth of the Rhine, Germany's main waterway. Along any of these rivers or the many canals connecting them look for the rectangular shapes of barges making their way around the country (see Transportation, page 41).

Also near the North Sea, keep an eye out for the telltale rows of long metal sheds and dark effluent of industrial animal husbandry. Evolving from a grazing past, this region of Germany has become an important livestock-raising center—but not because of any agricultural advantage. Indeed the land here is not suitable for much farming, but its proximity to North Sea ports affords easy access to cheap imported grain—the chief feed for animals such as pigs, chickens, and cattle.

In spite of the industrious buzz this landscape has long exuded, Germany came late to modern nationhood. Up until 1871, when the German Empire (the Second Reich) was established, Germany comprised a loose collection of small states and principalities. As a result it has many different centers, with many different regional economies—just the opposite of highly centralized countries like France that have a single dominant city. Outside the urban centers, you'll also see countryside strewn with small towns and villages, many of which date back thousands of years.

Particularly in the south, which was not as developed during industrialization nor, consequently, as devastated by the wars of the twentieth century, look for ancient medieval town layouts. You'll see narrow, winding streets surrounding huge churches or cathedrals, as at Nördlingen in Bavaria, northwest of Munich, where you can also see the ancient wall enclosing the town. There are a few even older layouts still visible in the south, as at Trier—the oldest city in Germany, founded by the Romans more than two thousand years ago at the very edge of their empire. You can still see remnants of the orderly Roman grid in the town center. The Romans also brought their wine-making heritage here, the continuing success of which you can plainly see on the slopes throughout the Moselle and Rhineland: Look for tight rows of vines, green in summer or brown in winter, drawn like the teeth of a comb along the slopes.

Germany's dense settlement—eighty million people live here, making it the largest country in the European Union—is defined by its great rivers, which generally flow from the central uplands toward the north. The Rhine, in particular, plays a crucial role in the nation. Flowing 1,300 kilometers (800 mi.) from its sources in the high Alps to the North Sea, the Rhine is one of Europe's longest rivers, and the longest in Germany.

For most of its length, the Rhine flows through Germany's central uplands. This area of rolling hills, rocky outcrops, and ancient volcanoes is part of a belt of similar uplands that stretches across Europe at this latitude. As you can clearly see from above, the central uplands are quite fragmented and diverse, as they are the result of many different geological processes over the eons.

At the northern edge of the uplands, where they rise from the North European Plain, you'll spot a zone of very fertile loess—a windblown soil laid down as the glaciers receded at the end of the last ice age. This region parallels a broad east-west glacial spillway in which you might spot the Mittelland Canal. Running from near Berlin to the Netherlands, this canal serves Germany's agricultural heartland. You can't help but notice how the rich farmland defines the landscape here—it's an endless vista of prosperous fields and farm towns.

In the uplands you'll see quite a few heavily forested regions. Virtually all of Germany was once covered in mixed deciduous woodlands, but most of it has been cut down since the fall of the Roman Empire. One of the first countries to run out of wood as its industrial economy developed, Germany became the home of modern forestry, the science of stewarding forestlands to continually grow trees. As a result, though little of the land is forested, Germany is continually one of Europe's top producers of wood and pulp. When you see dense, dark stands of trees of uniform height, often in rectangular plots, you're looking at tree plantations—the natural forest here has trees of many kinds and sizes, including many deciduous trees (characterized by a more rounded shape, and are of course bare in the winter).

But it is Germany's manufacturing heritage that makes it one of the world's top economies. A broad crescent of production centers that stretches from Düsseldorf to Dresden follows the nation's richest coal seams—the prerequisite for early industrialization. The Ruhr valley, in the west, houses Germany's industrial center. As you fly above it you'll see many factories, both old and new. At the opposite end of this crescent, in Saxony, you'll find a similarly industrialized area, but in considerably worse repair because of its Communist history.

THE RHINELAND: The Rhine flows across its broad plain near Darmstadt. You can clearly see the old meandering river course, as well as old sections of river that have become oxbow lakes, marshes, and farmland. The process of constant destruction and renewal has been interrupted by channelization, as in the center of this image. Straightening the river makes navigation easier, but it also makes the river more prone to flooding. Note that the fields are smaller along the ridge at the left: Protected from flooding, they conform to boundaries established long ago, while the boundaries along the river are more recent. Also note the forest at the lower right: It is a patchwork of squarish tree plantations—all the trees in each patch are the same type and age. Germany is the home of scientific forestry, and though most of the original forest is gone, the woods that remain are intensively managed.

Around the world, the concentration of industry and its need for a nearby workforce have created zones of continuous urbanization. Such belts, in which once-distinct cities merge into one another to create immense urban aggregations, were christened "megalopolises" in 1961 by French geographer Jean Gottman.

The Ruhr, seen here, was a valley of rural farmland as recently as the mid-nineteenth century. The discovery of high-quality coal in the valley led to rapid urbanization, with all its attendant problems. At one time, the Ruhr was one of the most polluted places in Europe, but changes in economic patterns and manufacturing processes have made it considerably less dirty today.

Together with the nearby Rhine conurbation, the Rhine-Ruhr megalopolis is home to some thirteen million people, making it the fourth-largest urban area in Europe. The nearby Rotterdam-Amsterdam megacity, known as Randstad Holland (see page 51), houses a further seven million people. In turn, this agglomeration connects to the south with urbanized Belgium, making this corner of Europe one of the most densely populated areas in the world.

Other European megalopolises include the Greater London Area, the Paris metropolitan region, and Greater Moscow. These belts of continuous urbanization are both a cause and a consequence of Europe's status as one of the most urban regions on Earth.

THE RUHR: The tangle of urbanization where the Ruhr (the smaller river here) joins the Rhine is a classic megalopolis. Dozens of towns and cities merge into one another to create an unbroken urban landscape with multiple, indistinct centers like Dortmund, Essen, and Duisburg, seen here. This kind of region is an unintentional twentieth-century invention: A mining and manufacturing region that evolved into a service and transportation nebula—something new in all of human history that is now the setting for the lives of hundreds of millions of people around the world. Twenty million people live within a two-hour drive of this spot, six million of them within the Ruhr proper.

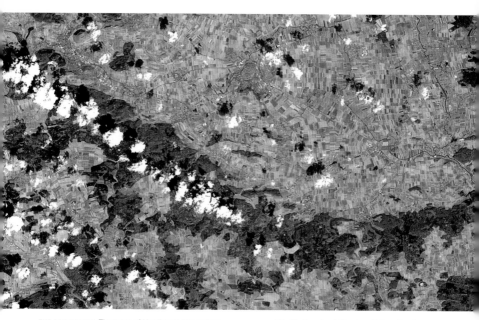

THE REIS CRATER: The town of Nordlingen in southern Germany is at the center of a crater caused by the impact of a meteorite 15 million years ago. Bits of characteristic rock resulting from this impact have been found strewn about Europe, especially in the Czech Republic. The distinctive circle of wooded hills outlines the rim of the crater. The flat basin inside the crater is 20 kilometers (12.4 mi.) across and is an area of fertile farmland. The town's location in the middle of the crater is no accident: The economic center of the area is most efficiently located in the geographical center. The pattern of farms centered on Nordlingen accentuates the bull's eye further: A rock falling from space determined how the country-side would be arranged.

The division between East and West Germany following World War II didn't follow geographical lines. Instead, it corresponded to lines between territories held by armies from different nations. Historically, of course, East and West had been interlocked, with countless roads, railways, canals, and rivers connecting them. The era of the artificial division of Germany into two parallel nations allowed the direct comparison of development under two competing systems—social democracy in the West and communism in the East. If you fly over both the Ruhr and Saxony, you'll get a chance to compare the results. More than fifteen years after reunification in 1990, evidence of the East's suffering remains visible from above. Under the sort of ruinous centralized economic system that once held sway from East Germany clear to the Pacific Ocean, entire industrial cities were created by sheer force of policy, rather than the dictates of economics. Eisenhüttenstadt on the Neisse River, the border with Poland, for example, was established in 1961 as a smelting city, where it commenced to pollute both air and water without clear economic purpose. Today, the steel plant has been refurbished by a Western steel company, which rescued it from being shut down completely, leaving the city's rigid grid, broad streets, and geometric clusters of apartment buildings to tell the distinctive story of a Communist planned city (see Central Planning, page 146).

But while the East German government was developing misguided showpieces like Eisenhüttenstadt, it also allowed critical infrastructure like the country's formerly extensive network of autobahns and railways to decay due to

THE IRON CURTAIN: Nearly twenty years after the end of the Cold War, the Iron Curtain is still visible across Europe. Here, on the North German Plain about halfway between Berlin and Hamburg, an angular clearing through the forest marks the old boundary between East and West, where American and Soviet forces once stared one another down, always moments away from launching unspeakable destruction. This sharp line demarcates more subtle differences, too: on the east, where the Communist government had collectivized agriculture, the farms remain larger than in the west, at the top left, even though they are no longer collectives. The large kettle pond in the middle of this image is the Arendsee, which, since reunification, regained its traditional role as a popular spot for summertime freshwater fun.

SPRAWL: American-style suburban sprawl rolls across farmland outside Leipzig. Unusual for Europe, where town planning and zoning are strictly controlled, this mode of development has appeared in some parts of the East where rapid economic development, combined with lax regulation, has resulted in a capital-driven free-for-all. Leipzig, located near prosperous centers of the former West Germany, is perhaps the most striking example of this. In this image, Porshe and BMW factories serve as a development pole that attracts sprawl in the form of office parks, subdivisions, malls, golf courses, and highways from the old city center off the bottom of the view.

lack of maintenance. Look for ghost autobahns—long ridges of abandoned highway that are a distinctively modern sort of ruin.

Poor central planning also devastated the environment. Throughout Saxony you'll see the yawning scars of open-pit mines where coal was once extracted. The region's low-quality, smoky coal was burned in facilities without pollution controls, blackening the skies of Saxony and resulting in respiratory diseases and powerful acid rain that has decimated the region's forests.

Since reunification, Germany has poured an estimated 1.5 trillion euros into the redevelopment of the East. Nonetheless, you'll still see plenty of evidence of the Cold War period on the land here, and the region continues to struggle—a daunting example from the point of view of other, less fortunate former Eastern Bloc countries that lack both a strong economic heritage and a lavishly generous national benefactor.

But the unfortunate East isn't just an example of the downside of central planning—it also exhibits some of the problems with laissez-faire capitalism. From the air you can see signs of uncontrolled growth. With chaotic regulations and money rushing in quickly, initial redevelopment in the East has been haphazard. Outside Berlin and Leipzig, for example, look for the kind of sprawl common to North America but rarely seen in Europe outside Spain: suburban developments, large shopping malls, and office parks gobbling up farmland.

As you move south, you'll see that Germany's Alpine region is distinct from the rest of the country. It rises slowly south of the Danube, which drains a broad plain of glacial outwash swept from the mountains to the south during the last ice age. Unlike the rest of Germany's rivers, the Danube flows eastward. You'll notice that the farms here are smaller than their counterparts in northern Germany. Here, different inheritance laws meant that parcels of land were more frequently split among heirs. In eastern Germany, collectivization created huge farms—much bigger than anything you'll see in the west or south, but common in other former Communist lands farther east. With reunification, many of these collectives were all but abandoned as people moved to more prosperous cities and areas in the west.

At the very south of Germany, the mountains rise into the foothills of the Alps and finally the Alps themselves. This area was long considered a backward and undeveloped part of Germany. But with modern transportation links and an advanced national economy no longer linked to coal deposits, the beautiful landscape and high standard of living have attracted a vibrant high-tech and service sector. Today this is one of Germany's fastest-growing regions. The new Munich airport, which there's a good chance you'll be passing through if you're flying here, epitomizes this new Germany: Sleek and efficient, it is like a computerized dreamscape and a far cry from the heavy image of the Ruhr or depressed Saxony.

While Europe is generally regarded as highly cultured and civilized, its history has been punctuated by outbursts of warfare so regularly that attacking one another seems to be a natural mode of interaction among European countries. Wars dating back thousands of years and others just decades ago have killed millions here and have left a profound mark on the land.

The direct impacts of warfare—bomb craters, ruined cities, refugee camps—are most visible where war has been most recent. Your best chance of seeing this evidence is over the areas of the Balkan Peninsula that were once part of Yugoslavia. You'll also see old bomb craters (watch for clusters of perfectly round ponds) and trenchlines in areas where the heavily mechanized world wars unfolded, notably France and Germany.

Evidence of the Cold War is widespread throughout Europe in the form of superpower military bases—some still occupied. In Europe, the largest American base is Ramstein, near Frankfurt, which hosts thirty-four thousand personnel and their families—a third of the total U.S. forces in Germany, scattered across forty-four bases. If you pass through the Frankfurt airport, you'll probably spot members of the American military—a living legacy of the Cold War and visible evidence of the diffuse American empire.

In Eastern Europe, you'll spot massive old Soviet bases, now abandoned relics—look for big airfields in remote places and rows and rows of uniform, drab buildings.

Ironically, some of Europe's military history has resulted in uniquely protected natural areas. Salisbury Plain in England, for example, has been the main U.K. training ground for the British Army since 1897. As a result, it has been spared the development that has overtaken much of the rest of England, and it is the last remaining substantial area of unplowed native chalk grassland in England.

Similarly, the old Iron Curtain—the militarized zone maintained by the Soviet Red Army along the border between Eastern and Western Europe during the Cold War—was kept largely forested while surrounding lands

TASZAR AIR BASE: As the front line of the Cold War, Europe is littered with military bases, the staging grounds for the Armageddon that never happened. Taszar Air Base in Hungary is typical of both Eastern Bloc and Western bases. It's clearly not a civilian airport: It is located in a remote area, and there is no terminal, no elaborate road or rail links, and no large parking area, yet the runways are wide and long. The bloblike concrete pads were for staging military aircraft. While many such bases are now abandoned, Taszar has simply switched sides: The base was built by the Soviets, but it became the main NATO airbase for the war in the former Yugoslavia and was the first base for unmanned Predator aircraft. Many civilian airports also house military equipment: Look for gray or camouflaged planes, rounded bunkers, and lots of helicopters as your plane taxis about.

were cleared. Watch for this long belt of forestland, especially in Germany and the Czech Republic. It is now becoming tattered, but efforts are afoot to preserve remaining areas as parkland—indeed, the largest forest park in Europe is in the Bavarian forest on the border between these two countries.

Warfare has been so endemic in Europe, you'll also see far older wars written on the land. The medieval town plans that you'll see throughout Europe, with their defensible locations (often at the tops of hills) and their fortified walls, are a picturesque legacy of thousands of years of near-continuous skirmishes. Even the Roman frontier towns scattered throughout the empire's former lands had such walls to defend against barbarian hordes.

BOMB CRATERS: The countryside of Polish Pomerania still shows evidence of the devastation of World War II. The patterns in the fields here are the remnants of bomb craters left behind as Nazi and Soviet forces squared off in the region. New craters are perfectly circular and often have a blossom of debris emanating from them. These craters are half a century old and have been filled and weathered to become more irregular. In areas of heavy bombardment like this, craters merge into each other to form a texture of devastation. The nearby town of Pyrzyce, a thousand-year-old regional center, was nearly completely destroyed. Holocaust and war completely altered the landscape here, and not just by leveling towns and scarring the fields: The depopulation of the area facilitated the development of larger farms than elsewhere in Poland after the war, as can be seen by comparing this image with the one on page 131.

THE ALPS

				GEOLOGICAL FEATURES	
				High, Jagged Peaks	Low, Glacial Valleys
				▲▲	⌄

			HYDROLOGICAL FEATURES		
		Glaciers	Snow	Lakes	
		△	❄	⬤	

				ECOLOGICAL FEATURES	
				Alpine Pasture	Evergreen Forests
				⋀⋀	🌲🌲

			HUMAN FEATURES		
		Ski Resorts	Farmland on Valley Bottoms	Tunnels	
		🎿	⌄⬠⌄	⌂	

BONUS SIGHTS

The Dolomites, the Matterhorn, Mont Blanc, Innsbruck, Liechtenstein, Simplon Pass

The Alps are the unmistakable mountain nexus of Western Europe. Comprising an arc of sharp peaks, this formation stretches from the Maritime Alps, bisecting the Riviera between Provence and Liguria, through the main body of the range in Switzerland and Austria and into the Dinaric Alps in the Balkans. This complex mountain system also includes ancillary ranges such as the Dolomites in Italy and the Julian Alps in Slovenia. Lower ranges like the Jura, between France and Switzerland, while geologically distinct, surround the Alps with additional highland areas.

This was the first mountain range closely studied by scientists, and many geological terms derive from place-names here (indeed, the word "alpine" itself has expanded to describe mountain features around the world). As the African tectonic plate moved northward and atop the Eurasian plate over the past 100 million years, successive layers of rock from ancient sea floors were folded and thrust upward, then sliced and piled into the ridges you see below (see Plate

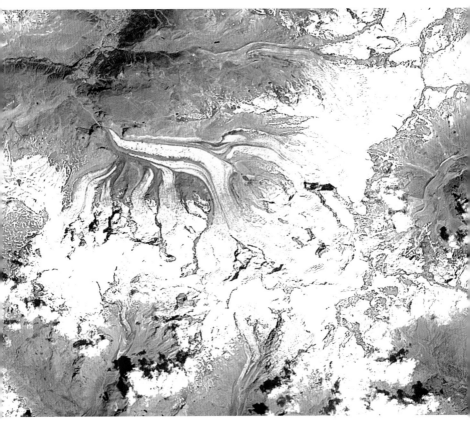

ICEFIELD: Glaciers spill from an ice cap in the Alps around the town of Zermatt, near the famous Matterhorn—a sharp arête formed by glacial action. This is a perfect spot to see how glaciers form mountain landscapes. These icefields are remnants of the ice sheet that once covered all of the Alps, forming the rugged landscape we see here today. The glacial tongues flowing down from the icefield in U-shaped valleys are surrounded by moraines and overshadowed by arêtes while cirques are being formed beneath the cap. And it might not be too long before we can see all of the effects of this ancient process: Icefields like this are today melting rapidly as the planet's climate warms. In Europe in particular they are an endangered feature of the landscape.

Tectonics, page 102). This seismic blender, still active, is the reason the Alps are composed of many different types of rock. From the air you'll see this reflected in the different colors of the mountains: Gray peaks are often made of hard granite, cream-colored rocks are limestones, and reddish or brown rock may be sandstone. Each of these originated in different ways, but all have been mashed together to form the Alps.

Much more recently—in the past two million years—glaciers have played their part in shaping the landscape, carving long, deep valleys and sharp peaks like the Matterhorn between Switzerland and Italy. As you fly over the Alps,

Virtually all the light you see on the ground comes from human activity—a life-size map of the human realm.

The density of light corresponds to the density of human endeavor, and makes visible the grand patterns of organization. Networks of roads and towns strung across the Paris Basin grow closer and bigger before finally merging into the City of Light's shimmering expanse. Lonely outposts shine in the High Arctic darkness with a single bright light.

The nightscape is a combination of points of white and orange. Orange lights improve contrast for nighttime drivers, are more energy efficient, and produce less light pollution—scattered, hazy light that obscures the night sky.

Other than electric lights, you may see the flares of gasses being burned off at oil refineries, landfills, and gas fields, and the occasional forest fire. The rest is inky darkness (see page 154 and 161 for more information about northern lights and lightning).

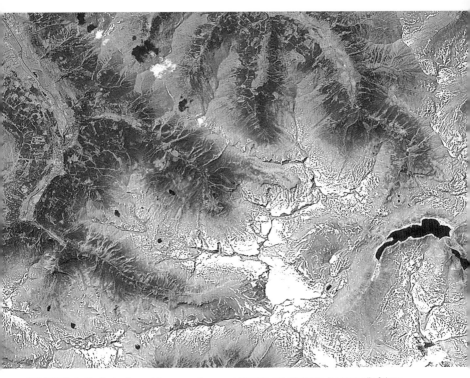

BAD GASTEIN: On the flanks of mountains surrounding the Austrian town of Bad Gastein, ski runs impart a cracked appearance to the forest. A major cause of forest loss in past decades, ski runs are of uniform width and meander down the slopes frequently intersecting with one another. In contrast, avalanche and rockslide chutes in the valley to the east of the town run straight downhill, tapering as they descend. They also tend to peter out, rather than arriving at parking lots and ski chalets. In winter, all of these features are strikingly white against the dark conifers. You may even be able to spot brightly dressed skiers making their way down the slopes. You can tell that the body of water in the lower right is a reservoir because of the curved dam and because of the line of exposed soil all around it, delimiting its high-water mark.

you'll see a repeating pattern of sharp ridges and deep glacial valleys (see Glacial Terrain, page 60). In some valleys, moraines have formed natural dams, creating lakes such as Lake Geneva in Switzerland and Lake Como in Italy. The shape of these lakes is characteristically long and narrow, conforming to the glacier's ancient footprint. You'll also see artificial reservoirs created to manage water flows and generate electricity—hydro power is paramount here. Look for abrupt fronts at the dams and more jagged shorelines than those of natural lakes.

Glaciers still remain, including several in the Bernese Alps in Switzerland that are 15 kilometers (9 mi.) or more in length. Look for extensive white snowfields even in the height of summer, and enjoy them while they last: As Earth warms, glaciers here are receding faster than ever (see Climate Change, page 82). This has prompted desperate measures to protect them and the economic advantage they bring as sources of both water and recreation; at Austria's Stubai Glacier, for example, white fleece is laid over the snowfield each summer to slow its demise and preserve the local ski industry. In other areas, ski resort operators aim to expand ever-higher into relatively pristine and cooler areas, angering environmentalists by developing the last of continental Europe's truly wild areas.

Together, these peaks form the roof of Western Europe: the origins of major rivers such as the Rhine, Po, Rhône, and tributaries of the Danube reside in the Alps. You'll soon see that many of the valleys through which these rivers flow are dramatically deep—it's not uncommon for peaks to rise over 2 kilometers (1 mi.) or more from nearby valley bottoms.

This topography has kept the Alps from being totally impassable: Trade routes running up these valleys and over the passes at their heads date back to Roman times and earlier and are still in use today. (Indeed, more than two thousand years ago, the great Carthaginian general Hannibal led thirty thousand men—plus elephants—through these mountains to attack ancient Rome.) Trading centers along these routes, such as the city of Zurich, grew prosperous as a result. The valleys' warmer climates and fertile glacial soils have long been favorable pockets for permanent settlement as well.

Traditional life here centered around livestock, and shepherds still take cattle and sheep into the high Alpine pastures each summer—look for swaths of green or gold above the forested lower reaches of the mountainsides. Inhospitable and snowbound in winter, these higher areas form an unbroken expanse of whiteness that brings to mind the days when the Alps were completely glaciated.

All these snowy mountains right in the heart of affluent Western Europe, of course, means that the Alps have become a major tourist region. This is the very birthplace of "Alpine" skiing—today a multibillion-euro industry that brings visitors from all over the world. From the air you can easily spot ski runs: Look for long corridors cut through the woods on the mountains' flanks. They'll usually radiate upward from a central nexus and are of course white in the winter, but green or brown in summertime. Where they come together look for ski lodges, condos, and plenty of parking.

You'll also be able to see avalanche tracks, treeless areas that, like ski runs, sweep down from the high mountains, but then end in forestland rather than hubs of human activity. In Switzerland, note that thick forest grows uphill from many mountain towns and villages. This traditional forestry practice, now encoded in strict laws, protects the settlements from the threat of avalanche. You may also spot the tracks left by landslides: Look for steep corridors of rubble the same color as the high mountains.

From the air, the relative wealth of different regions is plain to see. You can measure affluence by the evidence of human works you see on the ground. Denser and better-quality infrastructure—larger, wider roads, more bridges, more and bigger buildings—indicates greater wealth.

Farms, on the other hand, are not by themselves good indicators of the wealth of a region. For instance, large, post-Soviet collective farms can be very poor, while small French vineyards can be highly profitable. And conversely, large mechanized wheat farms in the Paris Basin are far more capital-intensive than small Greek olive groves. So in rural areas the best way to measure wealth is to look for evidence of mechanization—draught animals are a sign of poverty, while sleek new metal sheds, greenhouses, paved roads, and shiny tractors are signs of wealth.

Tall structures are indications of wealth simply because they cost so much to erect. Indeed, boldly demonstrating wealth and power was part of the impetus behind trophies like the Eiffel Tower, London's Canary Wharf, or Berlin's Fernsehturm.

Leisure is also a good indicator of wealth. Ski resorts, golf courses, marinas, swimming pools, and tennis courts all indicate a well-to-do region. Also look for how these facilities are kept up: Football fields with rutted and muddy or dusty surfaces show little investment in maintenance, while shiny new stadiums cost tens of millions of euros.

GENEVA: Geneva is perched at the tip of Lake Geneva, where this 73 kilometer (45 mi.) long lake drains into the Rhône River. Long lakes like this, forming in glacial valleys behind terminal moraines that serve as dams, are a distinctive feature of the Alps, especially in Switzerland and northern Italy. The landscape here, with its neat farms, dense road networks, multiple golf courses, and developed lakefront lots, reveals the prosperity of the region. Note how clouds are forming above the city—possibly due to rising air warmed by an urban heat island—and along the ridge at the top left, where clouds are condensing as moist air is forced to a higher altitude by the topography.

The development of a vigorous tourist industry in the Alps provides critical income for the economies in this region, for the land offers few natural resources and farmland is limited. Unfortunately, the massive influx of visitors—60 million vehicles enter little Switzerland (population 7.5 million) each year—has resulted in serious environmental problems. You'll see smog from automobile traffic plaguing the enclosed mountain valleys, especially near critical tunnels along major trans-Alpine routes. This smog has severely damaged the forestland here. Watch for layers of brownish air trapped in the valleys and mangy-looking forest cover (see Smog, page 168). Not only is this an unsightly environmental problem, but if the forests die completely they leave existing settlements vulnerable to avalanches, flooding, and landslides.

This formidable mountain range has also been a natural barrier between the different peoples living around and within it. The rugged terrain and high peaks discouraged intermixing and ultimately helped nurture distinctive cultures. Driven by the isolation brought by the steep terrain, the cultures in these rugged mountains pride themselves on their self-sufficiency and endemic customs. Alpine regions in predominantly lowland countries like Italy's Valle d'Aosta (just below the Alps'—and Europe's—highest peak, 4,810-meter/15,800-foot Mont Blanc on the French-Italian border) maintain distinctive cultures and even unique languages because of their isolating geography.

The entire country of Switzerland is an example of this phenomenon writ large. Though it shares languages—French, German, and Italian—with its neighbors, and is closely linked with them economically, Switzerland has for centuries been a country apart. Since the seventeenth century, Switzerland has maintained political neutrality, refusing even to join the United Nations and the EU. This doctrine originated at a time when to ally with any of its powerful neighbors would have meant risking tearing the country apart either along internal ethnic lines or by arousing the ire of other neighbors. Because of the defensible positions their mountain fastness provides, the Alps themselves have enabled the Swiss to remain neutral.

While Switzerland stands apart from the rest of Europe, other parts of the Alps are fully integrated with adjacent lowland regions. Austria stretches eastward into Eastern Europe's Hungarian Plain, and Slovenia, once part of Yugoslavia, has long been connected with the Balkan nations. In many ways, the Alps anchor Europe's diverse regions and cultures, forming an unmistakable geographical focal point.

CENTRAL EUROPE

WATCH FOR

GEOLOGICAL FEATURES

			Plains	Mountains
			≡	⌂⌂

HYDROLOGICAL FEATURES

		Rivers	Lakes	Marshes
		∿	●	.ᴠᴠᴠ.

ECOLOGICAL FEATURES

			Forests	Marshes
			🌲	.ᴠᴠᴠ.

HUMAN FEATURES

Farms	Cities	Canals	Dams	Mining
⌂	▮▮	⊨	▽	◗

BONUS SIGHTS
Prague, Warsaw, the Alföld, Transylvania, Lake Balaton

The countries between the former Soviet Union and Western Europe—Poland, the Czech Republic, Slovakia, eastern Austria, Hungary, and Romania—make up a protean region that's long been overshadowed by its powerful neighbors on either side. Historically, empires have come and gone here, and waves of invaders have left their mark on the cultures and landscapes of this heterogeneous area. Today the commonality of these countries is that, with the exception of Austria and the addition of former East Germany, they once formed the "Eastern Bloc" of Soviet client states in Europe.

Consequently, much of the present-day landscape—in particular, buildings, industrial facilities, and land-use patterns established in the postwar period—echoes Soviet models of centralized planning and massive agglomeration (see Central Planning, page 146).

Nonetheless, the regions here are quite different from one another geologically, ranging from glacial outwash to high mountain peaks to steppe and nearly Mediterranean scrubland.

Baltic Poland is part of the glacial North European Plain that stretches from Germany into Russia. With its low relief interrupted by sweeping moraines, this land of forest and farm served as the stage upon which the great twentieth-century struggles between these two powers were played out, much to the detriment of those living in Poland.

Today you'll see that this region continues to be heavily farmed, and it is notable that the agriculture here retains much of its prewar pattern: smaller holdings arranged haphazardly across the landscape. This is quite different from other parts of Eastern Europe. Farm collectivization failed in Poland in the 1950s while it succeeded elsewhere. Though this resulted in low agricultural productivity, particularly in comparison with Western Europe, it also left Poland with a traditionally rustic landscape of more than a million small farms at the time of the nation's entry into the EU in 2004. Preserving this landscape—almost a third of Poles work the land—has become a central part of the nation's tourism hopes and has also contributed to a boom in organic food production here.

Farther south, Poland, like Germany, rises through a fertile belt of loess (windblown glacial sediment) into the central European uplands, in this case the Bohemian uplands—the heart of the Czech Republic. As in nearby parts of Germany, this region features many large extinct volcanoes that you may be able to pick out from the air.

On the northern, Polish flanks of the uplands, Silesia is rich in low-quality lignite coal, and the land has paid the price: Huge open pit mines pock the landscape, and dirty coal-burning industrial facilities still darken the skies, though not as badly as before the fall of Communism in 1989, when this region was considered the most polluted area in Europe.

That dubious honor now falls on the nearby Bohemian Basin—the rolling uplands around Prague. This region is so highly polluted not just because of the many coal-burning industries here: Pollution floats in from Germany, notably nearby Saxony, as well as Silesia and even farther afield, and becomes trapped here. As a result the forests suffer the consequences of heavy acid rain. Look for layers of brown smog and tracts of dead woodlands—splotches of gray or brown forestland or mangy mountainsides.

South and east, primarily in Slovakia and Romania, you'll encounter the Carpathian Mountains. Curling in a broad arc toward the Black Sea, this range is as large as the Alps, although not as tall (the highest peak is Gerlachov Peak, in Slovakia, at 2,655 meters, or 8,711 feet). The storied landscape of Transylvania sits in the southern part of this range, in Romania. If you fly here, you'll see it's still as rugged and wooded as Bram Stoker described it in *Dracula*, although much more beautiful than you might expect from that dark vision.

POLISH COUNTRYSIDE: Unlike the rest of Eastern Europe, the Polish countryside was never collectivized. The result is a traditional landscape of small fields and villages. In the post-Communist period, this landscape has become a real asset as the country seeks to promote tourism in its bucolic landscape. Along with Italy, the nation has pioneered agrotourism, where visitors stay—and even work—on farms in an effort to get back to the sort of rugged connection with the land that urban dwellers feel they have lost (and that, as a result, it is easy for them to romanticize). This particular vista is in southern Poland, in the Voivodship of Opole outside the city of Katowice in Silesia.

The blocky lakes near the Oder are flooded gravel pits—a feature found throughout northern Europe where gravel, sand, and clay have been mined from the river floodplains where they were deposited by postglacial drainage.

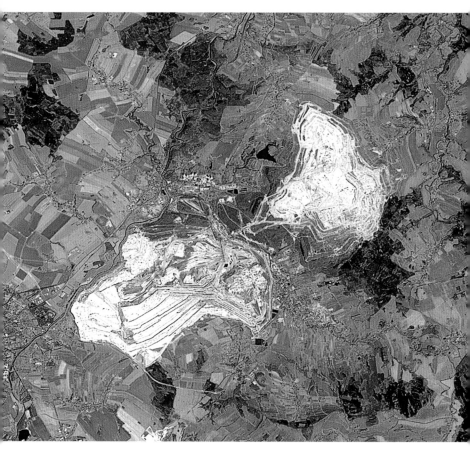

COAL MINES: In Silesia—southern Poland near the Czech border—strip mines dwarf nearby villages. A common feature on the landscape in a broad crescent from Belgium to Silesia, as well as elsewhere, these pits can be up to 10 kilometers across. They are a sign that coal seams—the fossilized remains of swamp plants 300 million years old—are close to the surface. In regions where seams are deeper, such as the British Isles and eastern Ukraine, mines are tunneled into the ground. While the low-quality bituminous coal beds seen here were responsible for jumpstarting the Industrial Revolution and formed the foundation of the Communist-era economy, they also led to serious pollution problems, including the acid rain that has denuded many European woodlands, as well as the global warming that Europe is confronting today.

Encircled by the Alps to the west, the Carpathians to the east, and the mountains of the Balkan Peninsula to the south, the Pannonian Basin in Hungary, Serbia, Romania, and Slovakia was a shallow sea filled in long ago by rich runoff from the surrounding ranges. The Danube and its tributaries water the relatively dry region, and the long, hot summers make this basin—in particular, the Alföld, or Great Hungarian Plain—a sort of natural hothouse. The produce—tomatoes especially—grown in the Alföld is legendary, and the region has long reigned as one of Europe's finest agricultural areas.

THE ALFÖLD: Mezőtúr sits on the Great Hungarian Plain, the Alföld. It is a regional center, as evidenced by its many transportation links, including canals and roads, and by the organization of the farmland around it. Though the farms here were collectivized during the Communist years, their basic pattern conforms to the much older system of roads and boundaries that have the town as their focal point: Even as systems of land tenure change, ancient patterns remain, and the town retains its role. Note the many small plots near the town: Many cities in Eastern Europe feature nearby garden plots where city dwellers can grow fruits and vegetables and escape the annoyances of city life.

The Pannonian Basin has been forever coveted by invading armies. In their time, Romans, Huns, Mongols (the basin was once steppe, like the Mongols' Central Asian home), and Ottomans have all included this prize at the margin of their respective empires. This is the heartland of the old Austro-Hungarian Empire, the dynasty that held sway for a half century here before the outbreak of World War I. Austria's capital, Vienna, still boasts the regal architecture and stately culture that characterized this dynasty and its predecessors. From the air, look for Vienna's distinctive layout of parklands and boulevards along the banks of the Danube.

In recent years Austria has rekindled its connection to the lands of Eastern Europe. Throughout the Cold War, it stood alone as a piece of Western Europe in the heart of the Eastern Bloc. Austria, and Vienna in particular, have been a natural entry point for Western capital moving eastward in the past decade, and the city has been booming as a result. Look for plenty of new

THE IRON GATE: On the border between Serbia and Romania, the Iron Gate is where the Danube passes between the rugged Carpathian and Balkan mountain ranges on its way east to the Black Sea. For most of history, the Iron Gate's fearsome waters were completely impassable to shipping. In the 1890s, parts of the gorge were blasted out so boats could be dragged up the raging rapids by locomotive. Since 1964, when the Iron Gate was dammed, a system of locks has enabled ships to pass between its high walls, making it possible for barge traffic to cross the continent from the Black Sea to the North Sea. The Iron Gate remains one of the most dramatic natural features in Europe, and the land on both sides is maintained as national parks.

construction here—towering cranes, gleaming new buildings—mirroring that in the major cities of the rest of the region.

The Danube itself is redolent with history. It acted as the northern boundary of the Roman Empire and, much later, served as the main corridor of the Austro-Hungarian Empire and the European gateway to the Ottoman Empire. This river continues to be a vital connection between Eastern and Western Europe. Flowing from Germany (where it is connected by canals to the Rhine and thus the North Sea), the Danube passes Vienna, Bratislava, Budapest, and Belgrade before flowing out of the Pannonian Basin through the Iron Gate—a gorge separating the Carpathians from the Balkans. If you fly here, look for where the unmistakably broad Danube flows into a long, narrow chasm. From the Iron Gate the Danube flows into the Walachian Plain, a low-lying fertile region that, like the Pannonian Basin, was once a body of water, in this case connected to the Black Sea.

With so many people living along its banks for so long, it's no surprise that much of the Danube's course has been heavily modified, sometimes with dire consequences. A massive diversion project in Slovakia became the basis for the world's first international environmental lawsuit in 1992 when the river course entering Hungary was reduced to a mere trickle. The Danube watershed includes parts of seventeen different countries and many industrial and urban areas, most of them in notoriously polluted former Communist lands. Massive spills, like the Romanian release of 100,000 cubic meters of cyanide-containing mining waste in 2000, as well as polluted agricultural runoff and untreated urban sewage have virtually destroyed the natural aquatic ecosystems in this river.

Nonetheless, the watershed still includes some important wetlands. Look for muddy, shallow lakes like the Neusiedler Zee straddling the border between Austria and Hungary south of Vienna (this area is a remnant of an ancient delta from the days when an inland sea filled the basin) or the long, narrow Lake Balaton a little farther south in Hungary. If you spot this lake, you'll be able to tell from the flat green carpet of reeds around it that much of it is a wetland rather than open water. This kind of habitat makes the Danube watershed a critical stopover for migratory birds traveling between Europe and Africa. Look for floodplain forest, river meanders, oxbow lakes, marshlands, long stretches of wide braided stream and, at the Black Sea, the Danube Delta. The Delta is the largest wetland in the watershed and includes the largest reed bed in the world. Though these represent just a small fraction of the original habitat, most of these wetlands are now protected.

Whether we're using an electric light, driving a car, flying a plane, refining aluminum, or making fertilizers, everything we do requires energy. It's not surprising that the massive infrastructure providing this power is visible nearly everywhere. The European Union is the second-largest consumer of energy in the world, after the United States (and after China, Russia is the fourth), and it shows from the air.

You'll see hydroelectric dams, which create large reservoirs of water (branching lakes with one flat end) in order to drive their turbines, as well as coal mines (open pits of brown and black) and oil and gas fields, particularly in the North Sea (watch for lonely platforms far from land).

From its source, petroleum is moved to refineries, where it is separated into useful substances like gasoline, jet fuel, heating oil, and the raw materials for plastics. Even though most of Europe's oil and gas are imported from other parts of the world, processing takes place largely in Europe.

In spite of its limited domestic supplies of petroleum, for example, Italy is the largest oil refining country in the EU. It hosts seventeen major refineries, like the one at right. Refineries like this are connected to tanker ports and continent-wide pipeline systems. Petroleum and natural gas arrives in Italy by pipeline from North Africa, the North Sea, Russia, and central Asia, as well as by tanker from the Middle East.

Electrical energy—the form of power we use the most for everything other than transportation—is generated at centralized plants. You can identify power plants of all kinds by watching for the high-voltage power lines that emanate from them. Watch for straight corridors cut through forests, up and over hills, and through cities and towns.

Another sign of many kinds of power plants are tall white towers in rural areas. Most thermal power plants—those that, like coal, gas, and nuclear, use heat to generate electricity—sit close to bodies of water used for cooling. These cooling towers vent excess heat in a telltale cloud of steam.

(continued)

1 mi

1 km

0

OIL REFINERY: The ISAB refinery on the island of Sicily—the second-largest refinery in Italy—is owned by ERG, Italy's largest independent oil and gas company (the company owns a fifth of the nation's refining capacity, processing 400,000 barrels of crude a day). The facility features all the classic refinery characteristics: Tank "farms" where crude oil and finished products are stored in huge cylindrical tanks (note the low berms around them to contain spills), pipes criss-crossing every which way, jetties for loading and unloading oil tankers (one ship is partially visible), and equipment for converting petroleum into things like gasoline and the raw materials for plastics and fertilizers. At night, refineries are lit up as though in celebration, and flames can often be seen as excess gasses are burned off. While providing jobs for towns like Priolo Gargallo, shown here, refineries are a mixed blessing: They are notorious for releasing dangerous chemicals.

NUCLEAR POWER PLANT: Noget, in operation since 1988, is a classic French nuclear power plant. The two white cooling towers and plume of steam are easily spotted from the air, although outside France they are not always sure indicators of nuclear plants: In Eastern Europe, in particular, many nonnuclear thermal plants also have (gray) cooling towers. Nuclear plants in Sweden and elsewhere may not have towers at all. The actual reactors are housed in the two rounded vessels near the towers. Nuclear power plants are usually near a source of water for cooling, as seen here. Like power plants of all kinds, they have a series of high-tension power lines running away from them, in this case out along a cut in the nearby forest. France is the world's leading user of nuclear power—the outcome of a decision made in the 1970s to reduce the country's dependence on imported oil for its energy.

The French Noget nuclear power plant in France's Champagne region, shown above, is one of the 204 commercial nuclear plants operating in Europe. France is heavily dependent on nuclear power. The country is the second-largest nuclear generator in the world, after the United States, and derives 80 percent of its electricity from this source. If you're flying over France, see if you can spot any of the country's 58 nuclear power plants, including perhaps the world's largest at Chooz. Nuclear plants can be identified by, in addition to the cooling towers, domed containment buildings that house the reactors themselves, as well as an absence of oil and gas storage tanks or the smokestacks that feature prominently at coal, oil, and gas-fired plants.

In 1986, an accident at the Chernobyl nuclear power plant in Ukraine spread radioactive debris over a swath of Europe that stretched through Ukraine, Belarus, Russia, Scandinavia, the

COPENHAGEN WIND FARM: An arc of wind turbines—the dotted line in the Baltic Sea—provides electricity for Copenhagen. Denmark, with its low profile and windy location between the North and Baltic Seas, is the world leader: A fifth of the nation's electricity is generated this way, by several of the largest offshore wind farms on Earth. Though half of the world's wind turbines were made here, other energy sources are also visible: Note the oil terminal of crowded white tanks by the water's edge. Wind has long been put to work here: Plans for the star-shaped Citadel Frederikshavn at the mouth of the harbor included a wind-powered gunpowder mill. One of the best-preserved seventeenth-century fortifications in Europe, the Citadel's characteristic prongs ("bastions") gave defenders many lines of fire and served the country well during its war with Sweden. The longer fortification on the other side of the harbor is now the green "Freetown" of Christiania, an alternative city established in 1971.

British Isles, and on to North America, causing tens of thousands of deaths over time. The eight-hundred-year-old city of Chernobyl itself is still virtually abandoned, at the heart of a zone too radioactive for human habitation. As victims of the largest-ever civilian nuclear power accident, Europeans have been understandably wary of nuclear power ever since. Some countries, like Italy, Germany, Spain, Belgium, and Sweden, have begun to dismantle their nuclear infrastructure.

You may also spot solar and wind power facilities. These are a little more spread out than other types of electrical generation, as you'll see if you fly over the fields of coastal wind turbines off the coast of Denmark. The six wind farms here generate nearly a third of the nation's energy needs—the highest proportion in the world. Nysted in the Baltic and Jutland on the North Sea are the two largest such installations on Earth—watch for rows of huge white rotors on spindly towers in the shallow sea.

With the exception of hydroelectric, solar, geothermal, and wind generation, all our modes of power production create a great deal of waste. From your window you'll see some of this waste as smog and plumes from smokestacks. With the vexing mixture of problems Europe faces, including the dependence of fragile economies in the East on nuclear power, the problems with greenhouse gas emissions from fossil fuels, limited petroleum reserves, and the challenge of long-term nuclear waste storage, it remains to be seen how Europe, and indeed the entire planet, will meet its voracious energy needs in the future.

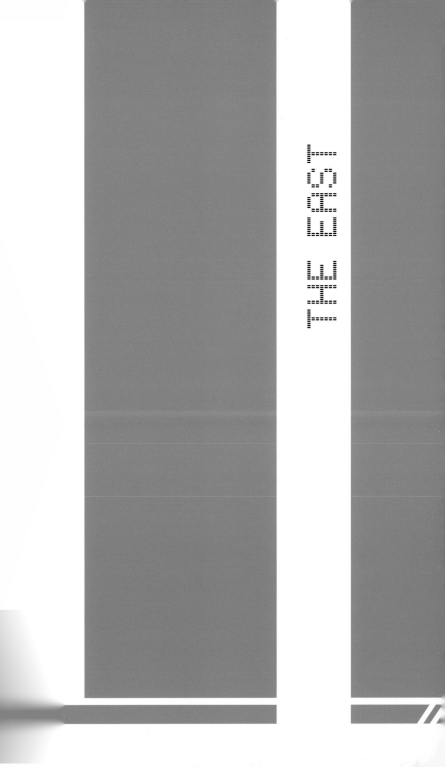

Murmansk

Saint Petersburg

ESTONIA

Baltic
Sea

LATVIA

LITHUANIA

BELARUS

Kiev

UKRAINE

VOLGA RIVER

RUSSIA

Moscow

THE EAST

DNIEPER RIVER

Black Sea

THE EAST

GEOLOGICAL FEATURES

River Delta	Moraines	Eskers	Loess Uplands

HYDROLOGICAL FEATURES

Reservoirs	Rivers	Glacial Lakes	Marshes	River Delta

ECOLOGICAL FEATURES

	Steppe	Taiga	Tundra

HUMAN FEATURES

Cities	Mining	Farms	Reservoirs

BONUS SIGHTS

Kiev, Moscow, the Dnieper, the Volga, Lake Ladoga, the White Sea, the Pinsk Marshes, the Curonian Spit, the Ural Mountains

Sweeping toward Asia, Europe's east—comprising the Slavic lands of Russia, Ukraine, and Belarus, as well as the Baltic States—is distinctively different from the rest of the continent. The vague eastern boundary of Europe is geographically often placed at the Ural Mountains, in the middle of the Eurasian land mass. Culturally, the boundary lies where the historic Slavic heartland grades into the lands of clearly Asian peoples. But both of these lines are arbitrary, highlighting the reality that Europe is actually an Asian peninsula, glamorized as a continent for no other reason than its history.

As elsewhere in Europe, history in the east, where the North European Plain expands into a vastness of glacial plains and ancient windblown loess has been deeply influenced by the land. With no insurmountable geographic barriers from the Carpathians in Romania and far western Ukraine clear to the mountainous regions bordering China, these low woodlands and rolling plains

BREADBASKET: The steppe of eastern Ukraine was once prairie. The rich, dark soil that these grasslands created is now used for intensive agriculture, especially of wheat on huge formerly collectivized farms. The body of water in the center of the image is a classic reservoir: Note the long, straight dam at its southern end. The rim of green around the reservoir is the range through which it expands and contracts with changing water levels.

were the arena for myriad epic historical struggles. From the conquests of the Mongol Hordes (the Mongol empire of the thirteenth century stretched from Hungary to Korea, making it the largest contiguous empire in all of human history) to the nightmarish struggle between the Soviet Union and Nazi Germany during World War II (more than forty million Soviets died in the "Great Patriotic War") and the horrifying internal terrors under Stalin, history here is as big as the landscape.

Without much topographical relief, the rolling plains of the East are distinguished from the air more by bands of different types of vegetation, ranging from Arctic tundra in the north (a treeless expanse of green, brown, or white, depending on the season) through taiga (dark coniferous woodland), mixed deciduous forest and grassland (green or brown with green trees in summer), steppe grasslands (green or brown, with trees only along river courses or where they have been planted), and semiarid scrub (brown with patches of dark vegetation). Farther east still, the center of the Eurasian continent is parched desert.

The climate ranges from the maritime-moderated Baltic and Black Sea areas to much more extreme continental heat and cold to the east. The heartland of this region—and of the former Soviet Union—is a heavily populated fertile zone that stretches from the Baltic through Ukraine and into the Central Russian Upland and the area around Moscow.

For centuries, this belt has connected the cultures of the Baltic Sea to the northwest with those of the Black Sea to the south. The ancient empire of Rus, the heir to the Byzantine empire and indirectly the Roman Empire itself, arose around Kiev more than a thousand years ago. This was the first articulation of Russian culture, but it was also the start of a millennium of bloodletting that has left deep marks on the landscape you see today.

Waves of invading Mongols drove the Russians north, into present-day Belarus and the area around Moscow. Moscow itself eventually became the center of the Russian nation. Located in the middle of a rolling rise in the glaciated North European Plain, Moscow is near the headwaters of rivers flowing in all directions. Both the Dnieper, which flows past Kiev into the Black Sea, and the Volga (the longest river in Europe), which flows into the Caspian Sea farther east, originate near Moscow. This location put Moscow at the center of important trade routes, helping it to become Russia's dominant city.

Later, when Russia began to industrialize, Moscow's position was solidified by the development of a road and rail network that placed this city at its center, like a continental spider sitting in its web. Flying into the region— and if you're flying to Russia, it's more than likely your first stop will be Moscow's Sheremetyevo Airport—you'll see that virtually all the major roads and rail lines for hundreds of kilometers around the city head directly toward it. Stretching in every direction from greater Moscow, these networks also include canals, pipelines, and power lines. Every part of this sprawling infrastructure points to the primacy of Moscow at the center of the bull's eye. No other major city in Europe exhibits such a centralized position in such a large network, a situation made possible by the absence of geographical impediments to sprawl.

For most of the twentieth century, from 1928 to the dissolution of the Soviet Union in 1991, the economy in the Soviet Union (and, after World War II, in central Europe) was "centrally planned." This system, wherein production levels and prices were fixed by decree, and the trajectories of new industries and their physical patterns were determined by bureaucratic fiat, was in direct opposition to the system prevailing in the rest of the world.

Almost everywhere else around the globe, then as now, capitalism held sway to varying degrees. Under most capitalist systems, the interplay of supply and demand in regulated markets automatically determines what products will be made and what prices they command. Capitalism, though regulated to some degree almost everywhere, was allowed to drive development in most other parts of the world.

The results of the era of central planning on the landscape of the European East are everywhere. Perhaps the clearest evidence here is the collectivization of farmland. In the early part of the twentieth century, the private holdings of small farmers and large landowners alike were seized by the state and converted to collectives, where rural workers toiled for the state on heavily mechanized, chemical-dependent farms. Look for immense acreage, often with central processing facilities like mills or rows of barns. Ironically, where capitalism and the free market have operated with the fewest restrictions, on similar lands in the American Midwest, the result appears quite similar from the air. In reality on the ground, however, the capitalist version of this process resulted in far more productive farms and less difficult social dislocations: While American family farmers were merely made landless and became urban poor, in the Soviet Union millions died in forced collectivization. Since the breakup of the Soviet Union, private farms have returned to the Russian landscape, but many collectives have become cooperatives that retain the Soviet structure and so appear relatively unchanged from above.

Industrial development was similarly planned here. In an effort to spread development to different parts of the country, particularly the east, industrial cities were created

(continued)

SWIDNIK: Though a village has been here since the fourteenth century, Swidnik, in southeastern Poland, is a prime example of a Communist-era planned city. In the 1950s, one of Eastern Europe's largest helicopter factories was built here. The concrete slab apartment housing to the south of the factory was built at the same time to house the workers.

In 1980 Swidnik became the birthplace of the Solidarity movement that eventually led to the end of Communism in Poland. Today, the plant still produces helicopters and is kept operating by

Western interests: It makes an insignificant part for U.S. Navy jets, as well as doors for Airbus. You may have passed by one when you boarded the plane you're on now.

Just outside the planned city, the landscape still features the distinctive Polish long lots, with farm buildings typically clustered along the road. With succeeding generations, lots often become narrower and narrower as they are subdivided. In a few cases here, these long lots have been further divided into tiny residential plots.

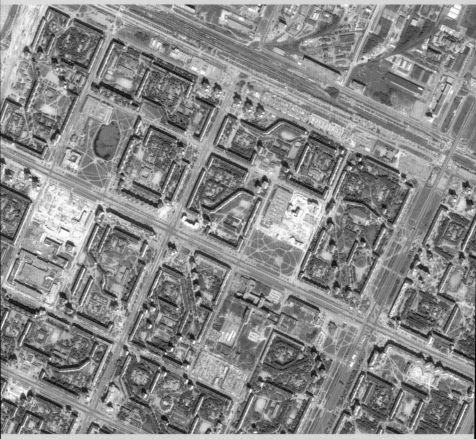

APARTMENT BUILDINGS: Prefabricated concrete buildings like these on the outskirts of Saint Petersburg provided cheap and quick housing in cities destroyed by World War II (18 million people needed a place to live just in East Germany). Though they often replaced squalid village or refugee camp conditions, their monumental facelessness proved to be deadening; the new landscapes inherently inhospitable. In some cases it seems almost intentional: The 1 kilometer-long apartment block in Gdansk, Poland, that is the longest single apartment building in Europe, for example, or the monotony of 13,000 standardized apartment blocks in Moscow. In the post–Cold War period, many of these buildings were abandoned—a million units in the former East Germany's "plattenbauten" alone still sit derelict.

Similar developments in the West faced the same problems, although planners there were not so dogged and had mostly stopped designing buildings like this by the 1980s.

from scratch at great expense. If you fly past remote cities that are densely packed with heavy industry, it's likely due to planned industrial development. Some of these cities were specialized centers for different industries, such as the secret "atomic cities." Around forty of these settlements were erected across the Soviet Union. Closed to all outsiders and their very existence officially secret, they provided the nation's nuclear armaments. In an industrial-era echo of medieval cities, these secret cities are often surrounded by a concrete wall—a giveaway from the air.

Conversely, you won't see some of the landscape features common in Western countries. The twentieth-century glass-and-steel modernist skyscrapers that invaded the central districts of cities such as Brussels and Frankfurt are simply absent from the formerly Communist lands. Any that you see today, such as those in former East Berlin, are post-1989 constructions.

The ideologically motivated central planners placed no value on a clean environment. As a result, the scale of environmental damage wrought by industrial society in the Soviet Union exceeds anything in the rest of the world. Regions of heavy industry like the Donets Basin just north of the Sea of Azov in Ukraine are full-blown disaster areas, where pollution has seriously shortened human life expectancy. Radioactive contamination around Chernobyl and other areas has rendered them simply uninhabitable. Rivers throughout the former Soviet Union remain badly polluted with sewage and chemicals—the worst in Europe—and even some very large bodies of water, like the Caspian Sea and much of the Black Sea, have been rendered ecologically dead. Strip mines and clearcuts mark the land willy-nilly, and oil spills, smog, and belching smoke blot the landscape.

While a centrally planned economy did permit the Soviet Union to bounce back from devastation after World War II and become an industrialized superpower, it imposed unsustainable human and economic costs. Since the demise of the Soviet Union, freer markets and (occasionally rampant) capitalism have come to this region. These lands are still undergoing the painful process of completely reinventing themselves with a different organizing principle.

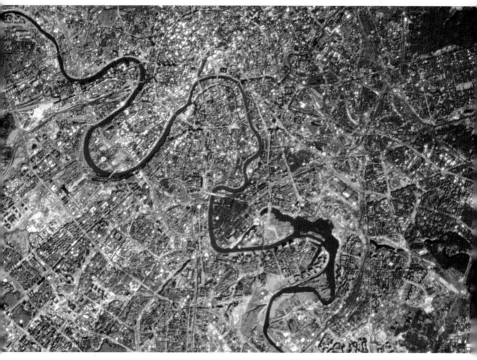

MOSCOW: One-tenth of the Russian population lives in Moscow, the largest city in Europe. This view of the city of 10.5 million shows the concentric nature of development here—a gigantic version of the rings of influence seen around many towns across Europe. In Moscow's case, the city's influence extends across a huge chunk of the Eurasian land mass all the way to the Pacific. As in many other European cities, the ring roads in the center of Moscow were built on the former locations of defensive walls.

Scattered throughout Moscow, you'll see a mix of industrial and residential development rare in Western Europe. Indeed, the lands of the former Soviet Union were industrialized under a markedly different system. Whereas in the West capitalist and later democratic considerations determined where industry was sited and how new development unfolded, development in Russia between 1928 and 1989 was centrally planned by Communist bureaucrats. The differences are clear from the air.

The Baltic States—Estonia, Latvia, and Lithuania—occupy a coastal plain that is still emerging from the Baltic Sea as the land has risen following the end of the last glaciation (see Glacial Terrain, page 60). These countries have historically been focused toward the West, their affairs intertwined with the other nations bordering the Baltic—a history that has been periodically interrupted by Russian domination.

Since the dissolution of the Soviet Union, the Baltic States have reverted to their historical Western focus, joining NATO and the European Union. Flying over this region, you'll see a combination of Soviet development patterns—factories in rural settings, for example—and newer Western features like shopping malls. You'll also see collectivized farms that have been redistributed to workers and former owners. Look for patterns of small farms within larger parcels that were once the collectives. In most cases, these smaller farms lack the mechanization that was once the norm on the collectives, and output has plummeted. While urban areas in the Baltics are thriving, the countryside is slipping backward. In summer, watch for old-fashioned hand-made haystacks dotting hand-cut fields. Though picturesque, these are marks of poverty.

South of the Baltic States lies Belarus, home to a people very closely related to Russians. Indeed, Belarus had been independent from Russia for only a single year in all of its history prior to the dissolution of the Soviet Union. The land here is low and swampy, particularly in the south, where you'll find the Pinsk Marshes. Watch for the naturally rust-colored water that flows from these wetlands into the Dnieper. Belarus, with its heavy-handed authoritarian state, is more of a holdover from the Communist period than any other part of the former Soviet Union—many of the restrictive elements of Soviet law are still in force here.

Ukraine, reaching north from the Black Sea and east from the Carpathian Mountains, ties together diverse regions: The nearly Mediterranean climate along the Black Sea grades into the continental landscape of the undulating loess uplands to the north, formed of ice-age windblown soil. The woodlands in the west give way to the grasslands in the east—steppe that stretches deep into the heart of Asia.

The western, wetter part of this grassland—in particular, the Ukrainian heartland on the banks of the Dnieper with its rich black earth—has become the breadbasket of the Slavic lands. As you fly here you'll see that it is heavily cultivated: The only unplowed land lies in the flood zones among the oxbows of rivers meandering across the plains. You can see endless fields of cereal crops—dark brown in the spring, green in the summer, and tan when the wheat is ripe in summer or fall. Early-summer-ripening wheat is called winter wheat, for it germinates in the autumn and lies dormant through the winter. To the north, you'll see fields of barley, flax, and potatoes, which thrive all the way into the subarctic regions above Saint Petersburg.

It is also evident from the air that these plains are well drained, with many large rivers helping irrigate the land as well as providing transportation networks that stretch throughout the region, connecting the Black and Caspian Seas with the Baltic and the Arctic Ocean. In particular, the Dnieper and the Volga are critical waterways. Both are heavily modified, with canals and channels to improve navigation and dams to attenuate their flows and generate hydroelectricity for the many industrial facilities in the region. For most of their

COLLECTIVIZATION: Poland and Ukraine face each other across the Bug River. The huge Ukrainian farms are the result of forced collectivization in the 1920s and 1930s that consolidated Soviet power here at the cost of millions of lives, both directly and by exacerbating famine. Collectivization was attempted in Poland, but unique among the Communist countries of Europe, it never got very far and the landscape today remains as it has for centuries. The underlying pattern of Ukrainian farms mirrors the clustering of the Polish farms because collectivization simply merged farms, rather than completely doing away with the existing systems of roads and boundaries. Large farms can theoretically operate more efficiently and with fewer people, but though a quarter of Poles work on the land, often using horses, Poland is now the largest agricultural producer in the EU while Ukraine's agricultural output is far lower than it could be.

length, both rivers are unmistakable from the air: chains of very long, narrow reservoirs that stretch for hundreds of miles.

North of Moscow, stretching almost to the coast of the Arctic Ocean, you'll see taiga, the boreal forest that extends into the Nordic countries to the west and Siberia in the east. This area is cool and moist, and for great stretches you're not likely to see much more than forest punctuated by occasional clearcuts (see page 62).

In the extreme north, Russia is washed by the cold waters of the Arctic Ocean. This is the coldest part of Europe, although it is even colder in Siberia, in Asia. Just south of the coast, the taiga peters out and you'll be flying over

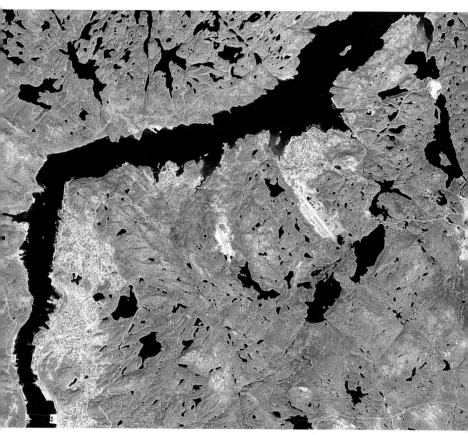

MURMANSK: With a population of 300,000, Murmansk is the largest city in the Arctic. Though the port is closer to the North Pole than it is to Moscow, it is ice-free all year-round thanks to the warm waters of the North Atlantic Drift. During both World War II and the Cold War, this was a strategic region for the Soviet Union. The closed military city of Severomorsk, featuring the long airstrip in this image, remains Russia's largest naval base. The area is also a major source of Arctic pollution from industries like nickel smelting as well as reckless disposal of radioactive waste (in addition to the 95 mothballed nuclear submarines scattered about the region, other sources include a fleet of gigantic nuclear-powered icebreakers). In this image, you can see that the lake-dotted, glacier-scoured terrain of the Kola Peninsula tends toward barrenness, an effect of the severe winters and short summers.

Arctic tundra. The treeline is the northernmost extent of continuous forest: the end of the taiga. Much as conditions on mountains become more and more difficult for plant life, leading to sparser vegetation as one goes higher, the colder weather of northern latitudes limits tree growth to regions south of this line.

North of the treeline you'll see the tundra—barrens of lichens, moss, and struggling shrubs that stretch to the Arctic Ocean. This landscape appears white and beige in the winter, green in the spring and summer, and red and yellow in the brief August autumn.

From here northward, the climate is cool enough that ice can remain in the soil all year long—solid water thus becomes a geological element called permafrost. Just a few centimeters below the surface and extending thousands of meters down, permafrost forms an impermeable barrier to liquid water, resulting in vast tracts of swampy wetland in summertime. These wetlands are the destination for tens of millions of waterfowl who fly here from all corners of the continent each year to raise their chicks.

Because glaciation was so recent here, and because much of the landscape is not obscured by forests or other plant growth, these latitudes present the air traveler with an unparalleled showcase of glacial landscape features. This is the original condition of many of the landforms much farther south that are now obscured by farms, cities, and forests. Moraines, eskers, outwash plains, and more are all on view here, in just-minted pristine forms unknown to the south (see Glacial Terrain, page 60).

The Arctic, technically that part of the Northern Hemisphere that experiences at least one day of total darkness each winter and one day of midnight sun each summer, is one of the most profound wildernesses on our planet. As you leave the mainland and fly out over the Arctic Ocean, you might see pack ice—a jagged white crust covering the water that at its seasonal peak in wintertime creates a contiguous landscape with the continent. There's rarely ice in the eastern part of Russia's Arctic thanks to the North Atlantic Drift, making Murmansk an ice-free port in spite of its location above the Arctic Circle. Farther north, the ice is permanent; this is the polar ice cap.

If you happen to be flying here during the polar night (winter), look out into the darkness and see if you can spot the aurora borealis. Also called the northern lights, these breathtaking sheets of green and pink high in the sky are caused by subatomic particles that stream out of the sun as a solar wind. These are pushed away from the atmosphere by Earth's magnetic field, except near the poles, where the field goes into the planet. Between 80 and 640 kilometers (50 and 400 mi.) above Earth's surface, the high-energy particles come into contact with gases in the atmosphere that release light as they are energized, much like in a fluorescent lightbulb. Oxygen atoms emit green light and nitrogen atoms produce pink, although many other colors are also visible, sometimes including a deep red from high-altitude oxygen, 320 kilometers (200 mi.) from Earth, on the edge of space.

THE SKY

THE ATMOSPHERE
CLOUDS
WEATHER

THE ATMOSPHERE

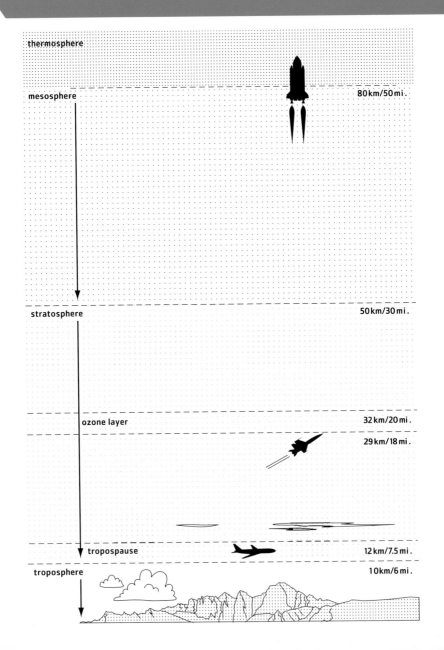

thermosphere

mesosphere   80 km/50 mi.

stratosphere   50 km/30 mi.

ozone layer   32 km/20 mi.

                                                29 km/18 mi.

tropospause   12 km/7.5 mi.

troposphere   10 km/6 mi.

The atmosphere is what makes it possible for us to live on the surface of this planet—and to fly over it! Gravity holds this blanket of gases to Earth. As a result, the air is denser closer to the surface: Its bulk is within the first 29 kilometers (18 mi.), which is why that is about the highest a jet can fly. There is also a very, very thin atmospheric presence up to 100 kilometers (62 mi.)—the height at which the European Space Agency considers space to begin.

This gradation in density is the reason your jet is flying so high: The thinner air between 9 and 12 kilometers (30,000 and 40,000 ft.) imposes less drag on the aircraft while still supplying enough lift for efficient flight. Best of all, these "cruising altitudes" put your flight path above the weather for less-turbulent passage. (For comparison, space shuttles usually orbit Earth at around 400 kilometers/250 miles.)

The atmosphere is divided into four main sections: the troposphere, to about 10 kilometers (6 mi.) up; the stratosphere, to about 50 kilometers (30 mi.); the mesosphere, to 80 kilometers (50 mi.); and the thermosphere thereafter for an indefinite and arbitrary distance.

The troposphere, where we live and where the weather we are familiar with takes place, is of the greatest interest to the air traveler. A transcontinental jet at cruising altitude is skirting the top of the troposphere in a zone called the tropopause, and is about halfway to the famous ozone layer in the stratosphere. This layer of gas absorbs ultraviolet radiation from the sun that would otherwise harm life on Earth. The ozone layer has been damaged by pollution, in turn leading to increased rates of skin cancer. Indeed, the atmosphere as a whole absorbs a great deal of harmful solar radiation and even at a jet plane's cruising altitude you are exposed to much more radiation than at ground level.

As you gaze down at the clouds below you on a bright sunny day, you'll notice a unique atmospheric phenomenon directly opposite the sun, surrounding your plane's shadow. A glory is an aura of bright pink and bluish bands radiating away from the shadow, or from the point where the shadow would be if it is not visible. This is sunlight that has been diffracted and reflected back toward its source by water droplets in the air or on the ground.

CLOUDS

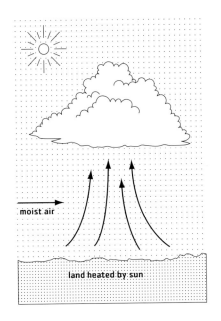

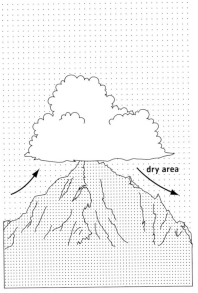

cloud formation

Sooner or later, as you gaze out your airplane window, you'll find yourself looking down on an endless plain of fluffy clouds obscuring the world below. Take heart in the fact that at least you're enjoying the sun, while the poor souls down below are suffering through an overcast day of steely gray at best—and take this opportunity to observe clouds from a new perspective.

Clouds are composed of liquid water and ice particles suspended in the atmosphere. Occurring in the troposphere and the lower reaches of the stratosphere, they are influenced by two primary factors: heat emanating from Earth's surface beneath them, and the jet stream winds above them.

A warm spot on the ground causes the air above it to rise. As air rises, it cools and thus loses some of its capacity to hold water. Water condenses out of the cooled air to form visible clouds. The type of cloud that develops varies according to local air conditions, which in turn depend in part on surface features and conditions and in part on the movement of air masses.

Since you're flying along a jetway—an invisible highway in the sky—you're quite likely to see the contrails, or condensation trails, left behind by other planes. Caused by the condensation of water into ice crystals as the hot exhaust of the engines cools, contrails look like billowy lines in the sky. With time, they are blown out into more natural-looking forms, particularly when the jet stream is strong.

Astronauts have reported that from space, contrails are some of the most readily visible evidence of human activity on the planet. They can be seen all over the globe, often radiating outward like starbursts from major destinations. Western Europe has, along with the United States, by far the greatest concentration of contrails in the world. This is a concrete manifestation of the magnitude of the air transportation system. You'll notice that contrails heading in different directions from your own flight will be at different altitudes. This vertical separation is a safety measure built into the system.

Trails that last a long time indicate humid air, while dry air makes them evaporate and disappear quickly. In extremely dry air, contrails may not form at all.

Where conditions are right, contrails can become cirrus clouds and can actually affect the weather. The absence of commercial jet traffic in North America for three days in September 2001, for example, resulted in clearer skies and greater ground temperature variation across the United States.

Cumulonimbus clouds often acquire internal electrical differentials as water droplets and ice crystals move within them, much as your body becomes charged when you shuffle across a carpet on a dry winter day. Lightning is the discharge of this energy between or within clouds or between clouds and the ground.

From the air, particularly at night, lightning is a spectacular sight as it illuminates the innards of huge thunderheads or spreads out across a cloud bank far below you. About 80 percent of lightning strikes within clouds, rather than between clouds and the ground, so from your high vantage point you'll see a lot of flashes you would otherwise miss.

Occasionally, lightning strikes an airplane, but not to worry: Because of Gauss's law, an effect whereby electrical charge distributed around a hollow metal object cancels itself out in the object's interior, people and electronics inside the plane are unaffected.

There are four broad types of clouds, each of which you can inspect close up from your window seat. Cloud science is a relatively new field: Clouds were classified into types only in 1803 by the Englishman Luke Howard, and it was not until the twentieth century when aviation brought them within reach that the dynamics of cloud life cycles began to be understood.

Cumulus clouds, the classic thunderheads, arise from the strong uplift of moist air, often on humid summer days. Rising up to 17 kilometers (11 mi.), they are the clouds responsible for much of what we don't like about weather: rain, hail, snowstorms, and, for air travelers, turbulence. They do look magnificent, however: These giant plumes of bright white vapor and ice glow in the high-altitude sun like mountains of cotton.

The life cycle of a cumulus cloud is about two hours. Young clouds have rounded tops, while more mature ones—those more likely to punish the people below with heavy weather—have the characteristic flat-topped anvil shape in which water droplets have turned to ice.

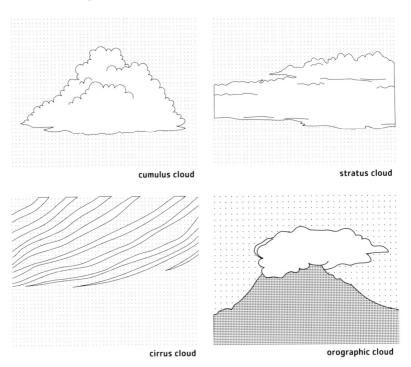

cumulus cloud

stratus cloud

cirrus cloud

orographic cloud

Stratus clouds, arranged like sheets in the sky, are caused by inversions in which cooler air prevents warmer air beneath it from rising. Stratus clouds form at the interface between these temperature zones and are responsible for the solid gray cloud ceilings we so often encounter soon after takeoff. By the same token, these clouds become the floor of our vista once we break through into the brilliant blue skies above them.

Stratus clouds can form in a wide range of altitudes, and they often occur as sheets of other cloud types, in which case they are called cirrostratus, stratocumulus, nimbostratus, and so on. Ground fog is also a form of stratus cloud, although one lying on the ground rather than floating in the sky.

Nimbus clouds are those fluffy, often rain-producing clouds found at low to middle altitudes in a wide variety of weather conditions. This is a catch-all classification that is generally no longer used by meteorologists, but works well for the casual observer.

Cirrus clouds, the high, wispy strands you find at altitudes above 5.5 kilometers (18,000 ft.) or more, are the only clouds that are likely to be higher than your plane at cruising altitude on a long flight. If they look a little like blowing snow it's no accident: They're composed of ice particles.

Orographic clouds, those resulting from air being lifted by landforms such as mountains, can be any of the types already mentioned, as well as a few unique forms. One of the most striking of these is the lenticular cloud. Shaped like horizontal lenses, these are very smooth, rounded stratus clouds usually associated with mountains in otherwise clear skies and strong winds. Keep an eye out for them especially on clear winter days in dry, mountainous regions. At times they may even be found forming over the top of a large cumulus cloud.

When orographic clouds result in rain or snow falling on the mountaintops, the air crossing the range is stripped of much of its moisture. As a result, downwind regions may experience a rain shadow. This is the reason the floor of the Po Valley is much drier than regions to the north and west: The Alps dry out wet Atlantic air masses by wringing rain and snow from them before they descend toward the Po.

Various combinations of all of these types of clouds can occur and are named accordingly. Examples include stratocumulus, altostratus ("alto" means high), altocumulus, and cirrocumulus. Whenever you see clouds that have characteristics of two different types—which is most of the time—you can guess at their names this way.

WEATHER

Weather is one effect of climate, a complex interaction between air masses, water, ice, land, and solar energy. European weather is primarily the result of air masses that move into the continent from predictable sources including the North Atlantic, Arctic, and Sahara regions. Weather generally moves from west to east across Europe due to high-altitude winds called the jet stream.

Blowing to more than 320 kilometers (200 mi.) per hour, the jet stream circles the planet 10 to 13 kilometers (6 to 8 mi.) above the surface. In the process, the jet stream pushes air masses along beneath it—and complicates air travel. These winds are the reason a flight from London to Moscow may take less time than the reverse flight. The jet stream meanders like a river so, while it generally pushes air masses from west to east, it can also push cold Arctic air south and hot African air northward. Flights are routed to avoid headwinds and take advantage of tailwinds in order to save fuel (and therefore money), so your route across the continent can be very different depending on which direction you are heading.

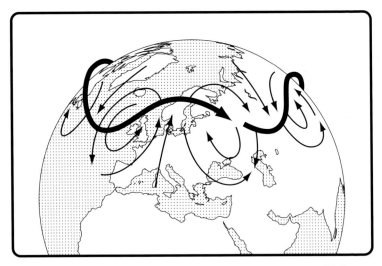

jet streams

Because weather, particularly the formation of clouds, is influenced by ground conditions, human activity can affect it in many ways. Particulates released into the air by human activity are not only visible in their own right, they can also stimulate cloud formation. The industrial activity in the Ruhr, for example, contributes to the general cloudiness experienced on the North German Plain by lofting pollution into the air that promotes the formation of clouds.

Other kinds of land use reflect and absorb heat, changing the amount of moisture in the air. One of the most dramatic examples of human-created weather is the thundershowers created by urban "heat islands." Cities are exceptionally hot because of their large masses of heat-absorbing concrete and asphalt and because there are many heat sources within them. Consequently, air often rises above these localized hotspots. As it cools, it can form thunderheads. Watch for stormy areas downwind of large cities, especially on late afternoons in the summer.

The color of the sky is so commonplace we often forget there is a reason for it: Molecules and atoms of the gases that make up the atmosphere (primarily nitrogen and oxygen) scatter blue light. Sunlight is made up of all the colors in the spectrum, and although the rest of them are able to pass straight through the atmosphere, allowing us to see the sun, blue light is scattered randomly from every part of the sky, making it all appear blue.

This property of the atmosphere is also the reason the sun looks yellowish or orange. Because the blue part of the sun's light has been reduced by atmospheric scattering by the time we see it, the sun appears a warmer hue. In space, where scattering does not take place, the sun appears white and the sky black.

Water vapor in the air also scatters light, but does so indiscriminately: All colors are affected equally, making clouds look white.

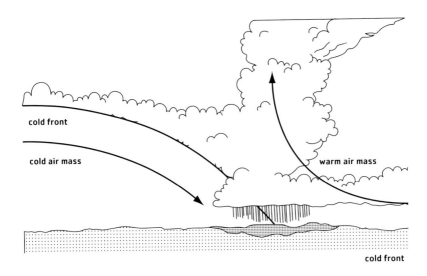

cold front

cold air mass

warm air mass

cold front

The air masses themselves are vast blobs of air with relatively uniform internal characteristics. The limbs of these masses—where they rub against one another—are the "fronts" we are all familiar with from weather maps. The differential between regions of air with different temperatures causes clouds to form at their interfaces. From the air, you can identify several different kinds of fronts and so determine the broad outlines of the air masses you are passing and imagine what conditions are like for the people beneath them.

COLD FRONT

When a cold air mass pushes into a warmer one, the cold air tends to push the warm air upward. This cools it and causes clouds to condense as very tall, columnar, cumulus clouds in a narrow line along the front.

Thunderstorms form in squall lines hundreds of kilometers long along advancing cold fronts, and are followed by enormous blankets of stratus clouds that form between the air masses.

WARM FRONT

In a warm front, the same thing happens, but for the opposite reason. The advancing warm air mass climbs on top of the cold air as it pushes it forward, again causing condensation and the formation of a storm front.

The first indication that you are approaching a warm front is a sky filled with cirrus clouds. Later, you'll see a blanket of stratus clouds. Closer to the front, you'll notice great masses of broad cumulus clouds, followed by thick stratus and nimbus clouds.

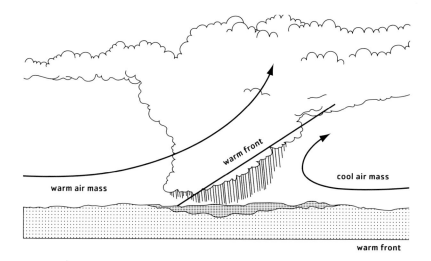

warm air mass

warm front

cool air mass

warm front

There are usually one or two air masses moving across Europe at any one time, so chances are good that you will see at least part of a front on any flight longer than a couple of hours. Whenever you see a line of cumulus clouds, it is likely you are looking at a front: the edge of an air mass moving perpendicularly to the line of clouds. If you have a newspaper handy, try to identify the front you are looking at in today's weather map and find out more about it.

One of the benefits of flying so high is that your plane avoids much of the rough weather associated with these clouds, although at lower altitudes storms can affect air travel dramatically. This is why the weather at the starting and ending points of your flight is so important, but bad weather in between is not likely to have much effect on your trip.

Still, a transcontinental flight is an inspection of a weather map in intimate detail—so intimate you can feel the updrafts of cumulus clouds and the usually invisible waves in the tropopause as your plane moves through them (sometimes these waves become visible as Kelvin-Helmholtz clouds, which look like a series of curling white ocean breakers in the sky). This wind shear—the interface between air streams moving in different directions or at different speeds—is what we experience as turbulence.

Smog is that sickening brown haze hovering above urban areas or other sources of pollution. It forms when there is an inversion—a layer of cool air sitting on top of a layer of stable warm air. Such conditions are common in basins surrounded by higher ground, such as the Bohemian Basin and the London Basin (where the term was coined in the nineteenth century to connote a combination of smoke and fog), but they can be found anywhere.

Pollutants, which can be from sources as diverse as factories, fireplaces, and forest fires but which are overwhelmingly from motor vehicles, become trapped at this layer, unable to rise or dissipate. Under the action of the sun, gases and particles in the pollution chemically change and become the visible miasma that has, unfortunately, become a normal part of the view from airplane windows.

The light of the sun is very bright and clear at high altitude. The thin air here lets it shine uninhibitedly on everything beneath it, which is why the clouds look so vibrant. Farther down, you might find that things look a little hazy, due in part to the density of the air there but also to the increased moisture and particulate matter—much of it from pollution—at lower altitudes.

Sunrise and sunset are particularly magnificent from the air. You'll see the light of the sun in the clear air while it is far below the horizon, and when it is low in the distance, it will light up everything with the resplendent glow that Earthbound observers can see only from a distance. When the sun is low, either just after sunrise or just before sunset, watch for a zone of darkness below you. Even though your plane is bathed in a warm glow, the ground below you is in Earth's shadow.

AFTERWORD

If you're reading this, it must be cloudy, or nighttime. Or perhaps you're laid over between flights or your seatmate has insisted that you lower the shade so she can watch that infernal movie about talking dogs. For whatever reason, you're presently unable to gaze like a heavenly being across the unfolding continent.

But at least now you know what you're missing, and are probably looking forward to your next flight. There is simply nothing to compare with the view we get from a routine passenger flight. It's the special treat of an impossible view, available to millions every day. As with many things in life, very few of us take the time to really see what we are looking at, and in the process we cheat ourselves out of the wonder and majesty of our world.

Learning to read the landscape from the air is just one step any of us can take to know our surroundings better; to appreciate more deeply Earth's immensity and beauty. Seen in this light, the pedestrian experience of taking a flight becomes a new and very powerful way to appreciate our planet and our civilization.

Now that you've read this book, I hope you will never again just glance out the airplane window—or any window, for that matter—and idly wonder what it is you are looking at before going back to killing time with a spreadsheet or an airport novel. You won't see just a mountain; you'll see the colliding forces of tectonic plates, millions of years of erosion, and buzzing human activity on its flanks. Your gaze is now more penetrating, and in better focus than ever before.

I hope that you take this spirit with you wherever you go and however you get there, for the magnificence of existence is all around us; we just need to open ourselves to it to feel its full force.

—Gregory Dicum

LIST OF FIGURES

GLOSSARY

arête – a sharp mountain ridge formed between two glaciers

barrier island – a long, narrow, sandy island formed by ocean currents and wave action off the coast of the mainland

caldera – a crater left behind by a volcanic eruption

cinder cone – a dark or reddish pile of lava chunks left where a volcano has spewed them out

cirque – a rounded hollow in a mountainside where a glacier once sat

collectivization – a Communist-era process of agglomerating landholdings under state ownership and working them with collective members rather than smallholders or casual labor

contrail – "condensation trails" of water vapor that form in the sky from a jet's exhaust

delta – a wide, marshy area of many channels where a river enters a larger body of water and drops its silt

drumlin (whaleback) hills – sloping hills left behind by glaciers; they often occur in groups, parallel to the direction of the glacier that formed them

esker – long, sinuous ridges that were once the beds of rivers that flowed under glaciers

estuary – an enclosed body of water where fresh river water mixes with salty seawater

fault – a seam or crack in Earth's crust

fjord – a long narrow inlet where a glacier once flowed from mountains into the sea

glory – a glowing aura on cloud tops around the shadow of an airplane

graben – a long depression between geological fault lines

heath – shrubby area, the result of thousands of years of human forest clearing and grazing in Northern Europe

hogback escarpment – a long, sharp ridge where a layer of rock emerges from the surrounding terrain

icefield – a small glacial ice cap

karst – a Swiss cheese–like landscape where flat limestone has been eroded by water to form many sinkholes, caverns, and underground rivers

kettle pond – a round pond formed by a chunk of ice left over from a glacier

levee – a long mound of earth built near a river to contain floodwaters

loess – fertile wind-blown soil laid in dunes at the end of the last Ice Age

maquis – dense Mediterranean evergreen shrubland, the result of millennia of forest clearing and grazing

marsh – a treeless wetland, including bogs

meander – the snakelike progression of a river, or a winding bulge in a river's course

moraine – a long ridge of sand and rock left behind by a glacier

oxbow lake – a long, curving lake left behind when a meander is cut off by changes in a river's course

permafrost – a layer of permanently frozen water and earth just under the ground surface that is responsible for many of the features in the Arctic and Subarctic

polder – land that has been reclaimed from the sea, usually enclosed by dikes

reservoir – the body of water behind a dam

sinkhole – the depression, often water filled, left behind when an underground cavern collapses

spillway – a broad channel where glacial meltwater once flowed

steppe – broad plains covered in natural grasslands

taiga – subarctic evergreen forest

tailing – waste rock left behind by a mining operation

tundra – Arctic or alpine habitat where it is too cold for trees to grow

watershed – the area that drains into a single body of water

INDEX

Author Biography

GREGORY DICUM is the author of *Window Seat: Reading the Landscape from the Air* and coauthor of *The Coffee Book: Anatomy of an Industry from Crop to the Last Drop*. He is at work on a version of *Window Seat* for younger readers.

He is based in San Francisco, where he writes about travel and the natural world. In addition to his biweekly column for the online edition of the *San Francisco Chronicle*, he has written for the *New York Times*, *Travel + Leisure*, *Harper's*, and others.

He would love to hear from you at www.windowseat.info.